# A Dozen Dead Roses

Tito L. Windham

A Dozen Dead Roses

Copyright © 2012 by Tito Windham

Dedicated to the Loving Memory of my two Grandmothers Ida Lee Windham and Sarah Catherine Wright and my Best Friend Antwain Evans! I know you are watching me from heaven!

# About the Book

In his 1st book, author Tito Windham tells the unforgettable story of a young girl who grows up in a sexually, physically and mentally abusive home with her drug addicted mother and step-father.

Born to a struggling single mother, Tonya is raped at the tender age of 13 by her step-father who is a strung-out on drugs. Most of her life she tries to escape the horrors that lurk with-in the walls of her home but finds herself deeply entrapped as a sex slave at the hands of her own parents.

She loses all hope for a better life until she gives birth to a child that renews her will to escape. At her darkest hour she meets her unlikely knight in shining armor that lifts her from the ashes that she had been buried beneath.

Filled with suspense, tragedy, romance and heroism, A Dozen Dead Rose is an unforgettable story about a dark world that so many innocent children throughout the world are trapped in and the power of fate to see us through our darkest days.

# Acknowledgments

I would like to sincerely thank and acknowledge a lot of great people who helped or inspired me to write this book but before I thank them please allow me to give honor and praise to the most-high God Almighty for blessing me with an unconquerable soul, a good heart, strong mind, powerful spirit and life. My Grandmothers, Ida Lee Windham and Sarah Catherine Wright, thanks for loving me and raising me as your own. You didn't have to but you did and I'm forever grateful.

My three children, you are my inspiration and the best thing about me. I love each of you more than I love life itself! D-Roc, you have an incredible spirit that inspires me and I love you just as I love my very own.

To avoid missing and offending anyone I would like to give a special thanks to all of my family, friends and everyone else who took the time to give me an encouraging word of support! Bob Rousseau thanks so much for your subject matter expertise in writing this book.

To my beloved fraternity, Omega Psi Phi and all Greek Letter Orgs you inspire me to want to be great through your continued efforts of service to others.

Thanks in advance to everyone who supported me by purchasing this book.

# Foreword

After reading this book, I am sure people will be wondering what my childhood was like. So let me tell you a little bit about it. The neighborhood I grew up in was called Kingston which later became known as the Eastside. Like most people who lived in Kingston we were dirt poor but my two grand-mothers did the best that they could with what they had to work with.

My childhood was far from perfect but now looking back on it as an adult I see we had it okay in comparison to other kids in my neighborhood. I grew up with my oldest brother Frederick "Fred" who was a few years older than me. At the time, we thought that not getting our way was a form of abuse but we were never actually abused in any way but I knew of kids in my neighborhood who were being sexually, physically and mentally abused by family members and trusted friends of their family. Back then beating a child with whatever you could put your hands on was not considered a reason for calling the police. So most instances of child abuse went unreported.

As I got older I found that I had a soft spot in my heart for children. Any time I would see, read or hear about harm coming to a child it would bother me. Once I became an adult and after the introduction of the internet I became aware of how wide spread child abuse was and how extreme some cases were.

I can remember reading news articles about children being chained to a pole in the basement for long periods of time, locked in freezers, raped, molested and killed by people who were supposed to protect and love them.

In International New, I can remember reading about the child sex trade and children being sold in to servitude across international borders.

Many of these stories in some way contributed me to writing this book. I was sitting in my apartment alone in Silver Springs, Maryland many years back bored out of my mind and I just decided to start writing short stories as a hobby. After about a week of writing I posted a few of my stories on a popular website and began to receive a lot of positive feedback.

Those that read my stories encouraged me to take it further and write a book. I dismissed the idea until years later I let a close friend read the original version of this story. After they explained how the story gave them chills I decided to finally write a book.

I never imagined I would write a book but once I decided I would, I knew that I wanted my first published book to be about something serious and very real. Being that I love children and hate seeing any harm come to them I felt it was on appropriate for me to make this story into my very first book.

Even though this book is completely made up from my imagination, let there be no doubt that there are thousands of children being abused all over the world. If you see or know of a child being abused be a hero and report it!

# Table of Contents

The Devil's Playhouse ................................................ 1

Coming of Age ........................................................ 7

The Birth of Slick ................................................... 29

Flesh of My Drug ..................................................... 51

Death of an Angel .................................................... 59

Motherly Love ........................................................ 83

A Supreme Summer ..................................................... 97

The Sweetest Summer Fall ............................................. 107

This I Will Defend ................................................... 123

Newly Born ........................................................... 133

# The Devil's Playhouse

It was about eleven in the morning when Tonya and her three-year-old daughter stood outside of the burning house, watching the flames stretch into the early morning sky.

She had been planning that day since the first day her drug-addicted stepfather cornered her in the bathroom one morning before school.

She had tried her best to avoid him, like so many other mornings, that day as she moved about the house, but this morning, he caught her off guard. When she pulled back the shower curtain, he was standing there with his trousers unfastened and a sick grin across his face.

This wasn't the first time he had tried to make a move on her, but this was the first time he caught her naked.

Almost a year ago to the very day, when she was only twelve years old, she first noticed how his eyes would follow her as she played about the house. He would sit and watch her closely like a wild hyena preparing to pounce on a young, defenseless gazelle.

Sometimes, her mother would leave her alone with him while she roamed the city streets in search of her next fix.

Before her mother could even get out the door, he would call Tonya over to sit on his lap and attempt to kiss her on the lips. She hated to see her mother leave because she knew she was her only line of protection from him.

Almost instantly, she would hold her breath as long as she could to avoid smelling the foul stench of his breath and body odor that often made her sick to her stomach. Even at 12-years-old, she had enough sense and natural instincts to know that the way he touched and looked at her wasn't right.

As he would explore her young body with his eyes and hands, she would squirm and try her hardest to get out of his grip, but his rough callus-covered hands would grip her even tighter, preventing her from escaping the monster's ill-placed lust.

Her stepfather was a frail, unkempt man with bad skin. Everyone around the neighborhood called him Slick, but his real name was Terry Parker. Terry rightfully earned his nick-name for his gift of gab and slick-talking ways in the streets of Jackson, Mississippi.

People that knew him would often jokingly say that he could talk a rattlesnake out of its teeth if he could get the snake to listen.

Since his early high school days, he made a living stealing, scheming and scamming people – mostly women – out of their valuables. Slick had done this for so long that it became second nature to him and quickly became his sole means of survival and income. There were times when he had a regular 9 to 5 like everyone else, but he would either get fired after getting caught trying to hustle his employer out of something or he would quit after he had hustled his employer out of enough to get him by until he could find another scam or hustle to run.

His ability to hustle was not the only thing he was known for; he was also known as a ladies' man around town. His sharp sense of fashion, good looks and Southern charm made him a magnet for women like Sharon Moss.

Sharon was a pretty young woman with a voluptuous body that drove the men in her neighborhood crazy. She knew she had body and she knew how to work it. By the age of 16, she had the body of a full-grown woman. By 18, she was the most sought after female in her community. Her mother didn't like the kind of attention her daughter's figure attracted and would always make an extra effort to ensure that Sharon was dressed conservatively any time she left the house, but her efforts were useless. Sharon had the kind of figure that could not be hidden, regardless of the kind of clothes she wore. Dresses, skirts, jeans or slacks, they all struggled and failed to contain her curves.

Unbeknownst to her mother, Sharon was also a hustler of sorts. She learned early, from watching the older women, that some men would do or give anything to get something that was difficult to get or forbidden. It was almost as if they couldn't help themselves, even when they knew what they were doing was wrong.

So, as she got older, she started using this to her advantage by using what she had to get what she wanted. When she was a little short on pocket money or needed a few dollars to help her mother with a bill, she would be sure to wear something form-fitting to accentuate her curves before leaving the house. To catch fish, you have to have bait, so she would show just enough to lure them in.

Since the age of 14, she had been working as a clerk at the neighborhood corner store where, nearly every day since she started working there, men would frequent the store just to get a look at her and flirt. Some were even so bold as to ask her on a date before she had even turned 16, but she would always turn them down because she knew her mother would have a fit if she even knew she was talking to the older men. Often, some of the men who visited the store would purchase small items and pay with big bills, just so they could say "keep the change." Even as young as she was, she was smart enough to know that this was their way of baiting her in by attempting to show how generous they could be. By the end of most of her work days, she would have at least a couple hundred dollars from all of the 'keep the change' encounters.

After a while, she became accustomed to men twice her age hitting on her and offering money and gifts in exchange for an opportunity to get some of her untouched goods. She never turned down the money or the gifts, but she never gave it up until she got involved with a gentleman by the name of Thomas Hardy.

Thomas, who went by Tommy, lived in the neighboring city of Cambridge, which was approximately 30 miles from the town of Greenville where Sharon lived.

Greenville was a medium-sized town whose population was mostly made up of hard-working medium to low-income families. Most of the people who lived in Greenville either worked in Jackson or one of the local manufacturing plants that surrounded the town.

# Coming of Age

It was during the fall of 1970 when Tommy and Sharon met at the annual Greenville Fall Festival. From the very moment he saw her, he was immediately attracted to her. He watched her closely, examining her from head to toe. The fall breeze had caused her dress to cling tightly to her body, revealing each and every one of her curves, much to his delight.

"Excuse me, ma'am," he said, with a big smile on his face. "May I ask your name?"

"Who's asking?" she replied, with a stern look on her face.

"Excuse my lack of manners. Thomas Hardy is my name," he said while reaching for her hand and bowing his head to kiss it.

She was flattered by his charm and gentlemanly ways.

"My name is Sharon, Sharon Moss," she said with a smile that covered her face.

For the next couple of hours, they strolled around the festival, locked in deep conversation. When it was time for her to leave, she took a moment to carefully write her telephone number on the back of his hand.

It wasn't before long Tommy put the number to use and gave her a call. For the next three weeks, Tommy drove down to Greenville every single day to see her and would normally stay as long as he possibly could without getting her in trouble. By the end of the first four weeks of their courtship and after a night of drinking, they made love for the very first time. It was a painful experience for Sharon, being that it was her first time, but she was eager to do it again as soon as she could. They started having sex regularly and almost every time Tommy came to see her, it would be one of the first things she wanted to do. The newness of it and the forbidden act of sex was very exciting to her, leading them to make love almost daily.

After about a month and a half in to the courtship, Sharon woke up one morning feeling almost like she was hung over, but she hadn't had anything to drink the night before. She quickly sprang from the bed moving as fast as she could to the bathroom. Just as she pulled the seat up from the toilet, every-thing in her stomach rushed up out of her mouth again and again until she was exhausted. She sat quietly on the floor near the tub almost in a state of depression because she knew one of her biggest fears had come true: she was pregnant. She had already noticed the changes in her body and appetite, but she walked around in denial until now. She sat there, staring at the wall, wondering how she was going to tell her mother.

The thought of her mother kicking her out frightened her, but her thoughts quickly shifted to Tommy and the possibility that he would leave her once he found out that she was pregnant. The very thought of him abandoning her to have and raise the baby alone frightened her even more.

*God, what am I going to do,* she thought to herself. *Tommy is a good man from a good family. He would never abandon me or his child she tried to convince herself.*

She was now feeling a little better about the situation, but still wasn't sure how her mother or Tommy would react to the news of her pregnancy.

For a second, she thought about trying to get an abortion, but in her family, that was considered the work of Satan himself. So, an abortion was out of the question. She was certain she didn't want to have the child, but she had come to grips with the fact that she really didn't have any other choice.

Sharon grew up in a God-fearing church home and getting pregnant out of wedlock was considered shameful and an embarrassment to the family during the 1970s. So, she knew her entire family would frown upon her sinful act of fornication and, on top of that, getting pregnant out of wedlock.

The following day after church, while her mother was preparing dinner, Sharon stood in her bedroom, building up her nerves to tell the woman who had given her life that she was now pregnant with a child of her own. She walked into the kitchen slowly with her head down. As the words left her lips, tears began to roll down her face on to the floor. The look of disappointment on her mother face was crushing and it gripped her insides. Before she could finish, without warning, her mother drew back for thunder and brought her right hand across Sharon's face with a sharp slap. Shocked and in pain, she struggled to maintain her balance. The sound of her mother's hand connecting to the flesh on her face echoed down the hall.

When she turned to look at her mother again, she saw tears streaming down her face.

"No, no, please, God no! Don't let this be!" she begged before dropping to her knees.

Sharon wanted so badly to rush to her side and comfort her, but she was afraid that she would be hit again. For nearly 20 minutes, they both sat in silence and cried.

When the tears stopped, her mother lifted herself to her feet and walked into the living room and Sharon followed. Her mother's look of disappointment was now replaced with a look of anger. She had not seen that look on her mother face in many years, but it was a look that no one could ever forget. She looked directly at Sharon for a moment without speaking.

"I want you out of my house," she eventually said, with anger in her voice.

"But, Mom –"

Sharon's interruption only angered her mother further.

"You have two weeks to find you somewhere to go. If in two weeks, your things are still here, I am going to put them out beside the curb and set them on fire. I've done my best to raise you right and this is how you repay me."

She paused and bit her lip.

"Laying up with a man that's not even your husband," she continued. "Like some kind of Jezebel. I'd rather be dead than allow you to bring your bastard child into your father's home. Your father is rolling over in his grave right now."

Sharon sat silent, as the second wave of tears began to flow like a river down her face onto her purple shirt.

After being verbally beaten down by her mother, she managed to retreat back to her room to escape the barrage of hurtful words that were being hurdled at her like a machine gun. Now that her mother had given her a two-week notice, more than ever, she prayed that Thomas would be the stand-up guy she had hoped him to be. She had yet to tell him of her pregnancy, but that day, she made up her mind that she would tell him the next time he came to visit.

The following Friday, like clockwork, Thomas drove past her house without stopping. He did this every time he came to let her know he had made it into town. As he turned the corner to park at their normal meeting place, he saw her already sitting beside the curb, waiting on him. Before he could get the car in park, she opened the door and jumped into the passenger seat. From the look on her face, he knew something was wrong.

"What's wrong babe?" he asked.

"My mother told me that I have two weeks to get out of her house," she responded.

"Why she say that? What happened?" he asked.

"I'm pregnant," she said, in a low voice.

Thomas sat silent for a minute before saying, "It's going to be okay. You can come live with me in my apartment. It's small, but it'll do for now. But, first, we have to get married because I don't want my child to be a bastard," he said, with a smile on his face.

She put her hands over her face to try and hide her tears of joy and relief, but her emotions overflowed as the river of tears began rolling down her face.

"Everything is going to be okay," he said, pulling her close to console her.

With his arm around her neck and his other hand on the steering wheel, he pulled the large car away from the curb and navigated it down the boulevard like a fighter pilot.

After about four blocks, he pulled in the South Inn Motel, where they got a room. For the next four hours, they made love like newlyweds and he enjoyed a few drinks to celebrate the fact that he was about to become a dad.

Sharon was still not excited about being pregnant, but she was relieved to know that she was not in it alone and that Thomas was a stand-up guy. After discussing the details and timeline of her move to Jackson, Thomas guided the car back down the boulevard towards Sharon's house. He pulled the car around the corner out of sight like he always did and gave her a final kiss and hug goodbye before watching her disappear around the corner.

It was now about three in the morning when Thomas started making his way towards the highway. As his car glided down the road, he reached to the side of the seat and reclined it back to make himself a little more comfortable. Then, he reached up to the radio and turned the dial until he found his favorite radio station FM 191.1 Soul. It was the Quiet Hour, which was one of his favorite times to listen to the radio. This particular radio program played nothing but classic loves songs until five in the morning.

At that time of the morning, there were hardly any cars on the road, so he decided to push the car up to 80 mph. He only had a short 30-minute drive ahead of him, but he wanted to get home as soon as possible so that he could get to bed. He had to be at work at seven, which only gave a couple of hours to sleep.

As the mellow tunes of Smokey Robinson filled the inside of the car, Thomas sang along as if he had written the song himself. At that very moment, it hit him. He was in love and soon to be a husband and a father. A big grin came across his face as he reached into his pocket for a cigarette.

*I'm going to be a dad*, he said to himself while looking at his reflection in the rearview mirror.

As the car reached the top of the hill, he noticed highlights coming in his direction. In an instant, a car speeding down the wrong way of the highway at 100 mph slammed into the front of his 1966 Impala, careening him into a wall. The force caused his vehicle to spin out of control and into the other lane, directly in the path of an oncoming 18-wheeler carrying steel construction beams. His car was almost disintegrated on impact from the massive amount of force from the oncoming truck, sending metal and glass flying into the early morning sky. Due to the severe impact, he was ejected from the car through the front windshield headfirst, sending him flying six feet into the air.

His mangled body dropped from the sky like a brick and hit the ground hard, bouncing his head off of the pavement. His skull cracked open from the impact, exposing part of his brain. His arms and legs were twisted and mangled with broken bones protruding from several different locations on his body.

Thomas was still slightly conscious and alive, but fading by the second. He could see his own blood draining from his body onto the road. His body twitched vigorously, as if he was having a seizure in a large pool of his own bright, red blood. He fought desperately to gasp for a breath of air, but his lungs and diaphragm were crushed, making it impossible for him to take a full breath. His eyes frantically searched the night for help but the way his body was positioned prevented him from being able to see anyone.

His car was smoking and nearly completely destroyed as it rolled to a stop against the railing that lined the highway. Debris, made up of twisted metal and glass, littered the highway in a nearly 50 yard radius and the smell of gasoline filled the night air.

The driver of the truck was dazed, but he managed to rush from his vehicle that was now on fire. Within seconds the truck was fully engulfed in flames. The bright glow lit the night, fully exposing the carnage of the wreckage strewn all over the roadway. Two more cars had arrived on the scene and were now rushing in to aid the victims of the accident. One man assisted the trucker to the side of the road and began rendering him aid. The other man ran to Thomas' car, searching for survivors.

"No one is in the car," he screamed to the other driver. Do you see the driver of this car anywhere?"

They both began scanning the area for any signs of a body until they noticed what looked like a ball of clothes about 20 yards up the highway.

"Oh my God," one man said, as he started running full speed in the direction of body. By the time he reached Thomas' side, he had already passed away. His eyes were wide open, but his body was now lifeless and fully covered in blood.

"Sir, sir, can you hear me?" the man yelled.

But, there was no response. He checked for a pulse, but was unable to find one. A feeling of sadness rushed over the man as he walked back to his car to find something to cover the body.

Out of nowhere, the driver of the vehicle that hit Thomas emerged from his mildly-damaged car, smelling of alcohol. He had only a minor bruise on the left side of his forehead from where his head had bumped up against the driver's side window. He was so drunk that he could barely keep his balance, as he stood watching the flames from the burning truck and all of the commotion that was going on. Seeing the extent of his damage, he quickly jumped back into his car and sped away, continuing down the wrong way of the highway, his taillights disappearing without a trace into the night.

Two weeks had passed and Sharon had not heard from Thomas. Their relationship was so young and such a secret, that she never got a chance to meet any of his relatives or friends.

At first, she was worried that something might have happened to him, but her worries quickly turned to disappointment and anger. The unknown allowed her to think the worse. Her heart was crushed at the thought that he had abandoned her, after all. In her heart, she allowed herself to believe that everything he had told her was a lie and that he had run off because of the baby.

A month had passed and there was still no sign or word from Thomas. By that time, she was convinced that he had run off to avoid taking responsibility for the child. This angered her to no end, which caused her to regret the baby even more. *If it wasn't for this damn baby, Thomas wouldn't have run off*, she often said to herself. This experience alone would forever change her life.

She never really envisioned herself having kids; to her, kids were nothing more than a burden and a nuisance than anything else. When people in the neighborhood would ask her to babysit their kids, she would always rudely decline their offer.

She dreaded the end of most days because she knew it meant that she was another day closer to her due date and yet another day closer to when she had to move out of her mother's home. After pleading with her mother, she was given an additional two weeks to find somewhere to stay.

She remembered overhearing the owner of the corner store where she worked at mention that he had an apartment for rent, but would only rent it out to the right tenant. Sharon knew that, with a little persuasion, she could get the manager to allow her to rent the apartment and that's exactly what he did.

With the assistance of a few people in the neighborhood and a few generous older men who were crazy about Sharon, she was able to scrape together some furniture and enough money to pay the deposit for the utilities. Her apartment was small, but it was the best she could do for the moment. With every paycheck, she would try to add something to the apartment. She first purchased curtains and then, a used television from the pawn shop. After a few months, the once bland-looking apartment started to come alive with colors, pictures, plants and the sound of a television and music from the stereo. She was proud of herself and what she had done with the apartment so far.

One Sunday, she invited her mother over for dinner, in hopes of showing her how well she was doing, but her mother was still angry and embarrassed by her pregnancy. During church service, she refused to even sit by her or acknowledge her presence. During this time period, having a child out of wedlock was considered shameful and looked bad upon the family name. Sharon's mother was having no part of it and this hurt Sharon deeply. She loved her mother and to be rejected by her was tearing her up.

Her resentment for the unborn child grew even stronger as a result. She felt she had lost her future husband and her mother all because of the baby. She was now huge and there was no way of avoiding the fact that she was pregnant. The morning sickness had stopped, but the extra weight and pressure of the baby made it difficult for her to get comfortable sitting, standing or sleeping. Most nights, she would toss and turn or just lie in bed staring at the ceiling. From time to time, she would find herself laying there, daydreaming about Thomas and the time they shared together.

The pregnancy was gradually wearing her down and it was becoming hard for her to motivate herself enough to go to work. Her feet were swollen from all the standing and walking she had to do at work. When she made it home at the end of the day, she would be so tired that she often fell asleep without eating sometimes. The lack of nourishment and sleep added to her feeling of fatigue. Her once well-kept appearance started to suffer.

Before becoming pregnant, she was a stickler for making sure her appearance was on point prior to leaving out the house. She wouldn't so much as walk to the mailbox without first checking her appearance in the mirror. Her hair was always combed and clothes were always neatly pressed and color coordinated. She wore just enough make up to complement her natural beauty, but now, she was often so tired that most days, she didn't even bother combing her hair, pressing her clothes or checking to see if what she was wearing matched.

Some of her regular visitors to the store had stopped coming by and when they did, they barely looked in her directions.

No longer was she receiving the 'keep the change' tips she had become accustomed to getting. Her self-esteem was now at an all-time low and she was nearing a state of prenatal depression.

Through it all, she managed to hang on and avoid going into labor prematurely. Right about nine months, on a stormy Wednesday night, Sharon's water broke. It was the 18th of July 1971 and she was all alone in a hospital bed, surrounded by strangers, giving birth to a child she never wanted. At approximately 7 pm, she gave birth to a 6 pound and 4 ounce baby girl, who she gave the name Tonya Renee Moss. Unlike most newborn babies, she came into the world with her eyes wide open and was as calm and quiet as can be.

After cutting the umbilical cord, the doctor held her near Sharon's head so she could get a look at her newborn.

"Congratulations, Ms. Moss," he said, before quickly handing the baby over to the nurse who began taping her on the bottom of her feet until she started crying.

The baby continued to cry as the nurse gently suctioned out her mouth and nose before giving her a warm bath to wash away the dried white fluids that covered her little body. After the bathing, the nurse wrapped her tightly in a small blanket and returned her to her mother.

With a big smile on her face, she said, "Congratulations, she is so beautiful."

Sharon reluctantly accepted her, but the sight of the pretty, little baby gave her chills. She was the spitting image of her father and had a head full of curly hair and dimples like her mother. The delicate, little flower slept peacefully, snuggled in her mother's arms as Sharon stared down at her with curious eyes. She explored her facial features and the way her hair came down over her ears. As she played with her tiny fingers, Tonya smiled in her sleep, bringing a huge smile on her mother's face. It was almost like she was looking at a younger version of Thomas.

*Where is he*, she wondered to herself, as she placed the baby in the basinet the nurse had placed beside the bed.

As the baby slept quietly, Sharon's mind drifted to thoughts of Thomas and the time they had shared together and the last night she had saw him. She remembered how good it felt to hear him say that everything was going to be okay, but that was a long time ago and everything wasn't okay.

Her heart ached as a wave of disappointment came over her. She felt all alone in a world where she would have to raise her child on her own. A child she never really wanted.

Three days after giving birth, she was released from the hospital with a clean bill of health and a brand new baby girl. On the day of her release from the hospital, no one was there to greet her or give her a ride home. After being rolled out in a wheelchair, she stood in front of the hospital with no plan on how to get home. She sat on a bench near the entrance rambling through her purse to see if she had enough money for a taxi. After a few minutes of searching, she was able to find about $60, which was more than enough to get a taxi home, but then she realized that she would soon need to purchase milk and diapers for the baby. The few diapers and cans of milk she had received from the hospital's starter program would only last about a week, at best. Tonya was only an infant, but already had a very good appetite.

She had no choice but to take the metro bus home from the hospital. She felt a little embarrassed to be traveling on the bus with a newborn baby, but this was an embarrassment she would just have to endure. When the bus arrived at her stop, she got off and made her way up the sidewalk towards her apartment. Before she reached her apartment, she ran into one of her neighbors who had helped her out from time to time with different odds and ends around her apartment.

He hurried over as fast as he could to assist her when he saw her struggling to carry the baby and the bags from the hospital. She was relieved to see him coming and was more than willing to let him take the bags. When they reach the front of the building, he put the bag down and took the opportunity to get a look of the baby.

He pulled back the blanket that was covering her head and smiled.

"Oh, well now, isn't she the most precious little thing you've even seen?"

Sharon smiled and said, "Thank you."

"So, what's her name," he asked?

"Her name is Tonya," she answered, before being interrupted by the sound of the man's wife, who was now standing at the entrance of the building.

"Don't you need to be getting to work?" she asked while giving her husband an evil eye.

She didn't even bother to acknowledge Sharon's presence until her husband turned to walk away towards the parking lot.

"Look! I thought I told you to stay away from my husband," the woman said.

"He was only helping me carry my bags to the door. I just had a baby and I was having a hard time carrying the bags and the baby," she said, in hopes of getting a little sympathy from the woman.

"I don't give a damn if you just had a litter of puppies. Don't let me catch you in my husband's face again or it's going to be a problem," the woman said, angrily before walking back into the building.

The entrance door slammed shut before Sharon could grab it. She shook her head in frustration as she started searching for her keys in her purse.

This was not the first encounter she had had with this woman. When she first moved into the building, the woman met her with a dirty look and has since given her a hard time every chance she got. Sharon was the only single woman living in the building and she was very attractive, which rubbed a lot of the wives living in the building wrong. They were very wary of her and made it their business to make her stay in the apartment building unpleasant, in hopes that she would move out.

This particular woman took a special interest in being as rude and obnoxious as possible, due to the fact that she saw Sharon as a threat. She didn't care for any woman being around her husband, but she had an extra dislike for the single ones.

It was nothing in particular that Sharon was doing to pro-
voke the wife's feelings of insecurity, but it was hard for most
men who came into contact with her to resist the temptation of
trying to make a pass at her.

Sharon, by nature, wasn't a fighter, so she did her best to
avoid conflict by ignoring the rude behavior of the women in
her building and the advances of their husbands. This, however, didn't stop the husbands from going out of their way to be
friendly to her every chance they saw her.

After unlocking the entrance door that was slammed in her
face, she made her way up the stairs. When she made it in the
apartment, she placed the baby on the couch between pillows
to prevent her from rolling off of the couch and ran back
downstairs to grab the bags she had left. Once she got the bags
into the apartment, she prepared to warm bottles for the baby
and a sandwich for herself and made herself comfortable on the
couch. She was exhausted and still recovering from giving
birth and all she wanted to do was rest and relax in front of the
television.

In seconds, she was fast asleep and instead of watching television, the television was watching her. It wasn't until she
heard the baby's cries that she awakened from her deep sleep.
She was so tired and the sound of the baby crying was the most
irritating noise she had ever heard. She reluctantly picked the
baby up from the couch and gave her a bottle of the formula

she had prepared. The taste of the warm formula calmed the baby's cries and before the bottle was empty, she was again fast asleep and then, her mother followed suit.

For the next month and a half, Sharon stayed home from work and only left the house to purchase supplies, food and diapers for the baby. The newborn was wearing her out and the lack of sleep, due to the baby waking up in the middle of the night to be changed or fed, had her at a sleep-deprived mental state of frustration

She was almost at her wits end and didn't know how much longer she could keep this up without losing her mind. The money she had saved was running out and the meager amount of public assistance she was getting was the only thing keeping them afloat.

Tonya was growing fast and eating more and more by the week. She was going through diapers almost as fast as Sharon could purchase them.

After being off work for what seemed like forever, Sharon was eager to get back in the swing of things.

She had found someone that would keep Tonya for a reasonable price and the owner of the store was happy to have her back. Though she was not happy with her circumstances, everything was going good.

Before long, the baby had become a one-year-old and it was a full time job keeping the little busybody out of everything. If she wasn't under the kitchen sink, playing with the pots and pans, she was in the refrigerator, pulling down everything that had color to it. She was a curious little baby that loved her mother, despite never truly being showed love in return.

Her very first birthday was like every other day of her life thus far. There was nothing special about it, except for the cupcake she got to eat while with the babysitter, which she devoured on sight.

# The Birth of Slick

Tonya was about two years old when her mother met Slick, who was a few years older than her. By this time, Sharon's body was back to her pre-pregnancy shape and just like old times, the men around town were back in hot pursuit of her. Her body was back to the old, but she now had a new state of mind.

Up until she met Slick, she never let another man get close enough for her to catch feelings. She now only saw men as a means to an end and that end was the almighty dollar. It was now strictly about business and getting whatever she could out of them. Her ultimate goal was to meet and marry a man with money, but until she met a man of that caliber, she would use the others to get by.

Now being street savvy, she knew that most men that had something going for themselves didn't like a woman who already had kids, so she would often leave Tonya at home alone or with anyone who would keep her while she floated about the city's club and party scene.

One night, while attending a birthday party at one of the local hot spots, she made eye contact with a light skinned, well-dressed man who seemed to have the attention of every woman in the party.

As he moved about the club, the diamonds in his ring and watch sparkled in the light, making him stand out even more.

Unlike most other men, he seemed disinterested in Sharon, which sparked her curiosity even further. She made her way to an open part of the club directly in his line of sight, where he could not help but to see her curves as she moved to the music, but still he barely glanced in her direction.

This was something she had never experienced before. Most men were climbing over each other to get her attention, but not this one. Her curiosity was getting the best of her and she just had to know who this man was. After a few more drinks, she built up enough courage to approach him.

"Hello, my name is Sharon," she said, while trying to compose her nerves.

"Hi Sharon. I'm Terry, but everybody calls me Slick."

"Slick, huh? Well, is it okay if I call you Terry?"

"You can call me whatever you like," he answered, with a light chuckle in his voice.

The ice was broken and the attraction between the two of them suddenly became mutual. Slick was a take charge kind of guy, so he grabbed her by the hand unexpectedly and led her out of the noisy club into the hallway so that he could be sure that his words where clearly heard.

For the remainder of the night, Sharon stuck close to Slick, captivated by his every word. Slick was a very charismatic man who had a way with words. She was immediately impressed by his sophisticated mannerisms. He spoke to her in a way that made her feel special, as he had done it to many women before her. She listened closely as he sold her a dream of a lifetime. The false tales about his exotic travels to foreign lands and the lavish lifestyle he lived sounded surreal to her naïve ears. Sharon stood there, gullible as ever, buying into it at full price.

Being that he appeared to have it together and didn't seem to mind the fact that she had a child, she was eager to make the most of the relationship. Most of her free time was spent with him, which, often, caused Sharon to neglect Tonya.

Within a month after meeting, he convinced her to let him move in with her and Tonya while they were supposedly renovating his condo. Not too long after that, he had convinced her that it was a good idea for him to keep her car while she was at work. Just like that, in no time, she was under his spell and pretty much everything he said, she did.

It wasn't before long that she was giving him money to support his different get rich schemes, or 'business investments,' as he called them. Before they had even been together for a complete year, he had already convinced her to let him manage the money coming into the house. So, when she got paid, she brought her paycheck home to him.

Unbeknownst to her, when she first met him, he had a slight drug problem. During his early days of high school, he had started experimenting with drugs and alcohol and, by age 32, he was a full-fledged heroin addict. The hustling skills and gift of gab he once used to get over on women and support his way of life quickly became his sole means to support his habit.

The good looks that had once lured the ladies in were long gone and replaced by monstrous, zombie-like features. His skin was now scabbed from constant picking and he now had a droopy posture.

Every dime he could get his hands on was used to feed to his hungry, junkie veins.

It wasn't long before Sharon was hooked on heroin herself. She had helped him tie off his veins many times and she stood and watched the rush of his high as the opiate flowed into his veins. Her curious mind would always leave her wondering how it felt and sometimes, when he came down from his high, she would ask, "How does it feel?" His response would almost always be, "Try it and find out for yourself."

For nearly a year, she was able to resist the urges of her curiosity until one late night, while they sat silently in the dimly lit bedroom, treating themselves to the last little bit of marijuana and vodka they had, Slick's rough voice broke the air.

"You love me, don't you," he asked, turning to look at her.

"Yes, you know I love you, babe," she responded, looking down at the floor.

"Well, why won't you get high with me?"

She was curious about the drugs affects, but was too scared to actually try it. Plus, she saw how bad he had started to look from using it. He had tried many times over the years to convince her to get high with him, but she always found a way to get out of it of doing it. This night, he was not taking no for an answer.

"Come here and sit next to me," he said, as he pulled out his cooking supplies and a small vial of heroin.

She sat next to him, quiet, and stared in fright as he cooked up his favorite recipe. The flames from the lighter glowed as the main course sizzled in the large silver spoon. His pupils zeroed in on the spoon until its contents were ready to be served. Like a master of his craft, he grabbed a used syringe from beside the bed and pulled the liquid from the spoon into the syringe.

Sharon had lost her buzz and was now terrified. She got up to walk out of the room, but he pushed her back down on the bed.

"Give me your arm!" he demanded.

She refused and pulled away. He responded with a strong backhand across her face that knocked her off the bed and onto the floor. Before she could attempt to get up, he brought his boot down hard in the middle of her back.

Hearing the commotion, Tonya ran into the room to find Slick standing over her mother. She tried to run to her mother's side, but he blocked her path with his legs. He dragged her kicking and screaming out of the room and slammed the door closed before she could try to get back in. After locking the door, he made his way back over to Sharon, who was now under the bed. He dragged her out by her feet and stomped on her upper back with his large boot. Her chest hit the floor with a thud. Tonya tried her best to get back into the room to help her mother, but door was locked shut.

He snatched her up from the floor and threw her across the bed.

"Bitch, the next time I tell you to do something, you better do it and do it fast," he yelled in a rage.

She tried to make a run for the door, but she was stopped in her tracks by the hard, roundhouse punch that hit her square on the side of her face.

Her face was now battered and bruised from the beating and she was too scared to resist. She lay across the bed in fear, as he tied the dirty piece of rubber strap around her arm above her elbow. Her constricted vein pushed up against her skins, making them an easy target. The needle pierced her skin and a flash of blood filled the syringe. He pushed on the plunger until half of the heroin was injected into her veins. As the drugs entered her bloodstream, she felt a surge of euphoria, followed by a warm flushing of the skin. Her mouth became dry and her arms felt weighed down. The rush was short-lived and she fell into a state that alternated between alert and drowsy. She tried to speak, but her words were slurred and slow and her eyes drooped down, as if she was falling asleep.

He sat beside the bed, watching the effects of his work before taking the rubber band off of her arm and tying it around his until his vein pushed tight against his skin. Relaxing back against the headboard, he pushed the remaining drugs into his arm. By this time, Sharon was completely in a coma-like state. Her body stretched out across the bed and her pupils dilated as she felt herself beginning to float. It was as if she was disoriented, but the feeling was so good.

From that night forward, the drug took control. She woke up the next morning to find Slick gone and Tonya kneeling next to her in the bed.

"Mommy, Mommy, wake up," the child said repeatedly until she saw her mother eyes looking back at her.

"What is it, child?" her mother said, as she sat up in the bed.

"Mommy, are you okay? There is blood on your face."

Before she could respond to her daughter she had a sudden feeling of nausea. The contents of her stomach were now boiling inside of her. She jumped to her feet and rush toward the bathroom. Everything in her stomach was now rushing towards her mouth and she had only seconds before it would be all over floor. She made it to the toilet just in time before she began to vomit. Tonya looked frightened as she stood at the bathroom door, watching her mother's body have a reaction to the drugs. Wave after wave of everything in her stomach hurdled out of her mouth and nose until she sat finally beside the toilet, exhausted.

She reached and grabbed the corner of the face bowl and pulled herself to her feet. Tonya tried to assist her, but she pushed the child away. After standing, she turned to look into the mirror and was horrified at what she saw. Her face was swollen and bruised from the beating she had taken. She felt ashamed of how she now looked. Her hair was wild all over her head and she had bruises on her arms, chest, face and neck. Her lip was split in two and her right eye was blackened. She felt a burning sensation where the needle had pierced her veins. Her entire body felt sore, especially her back, as she staggered back into the bedroom. The child followed behind her, but was careful to keep a safe distance.

Sharon made her way back to the side of the bed and began searching the nightstand for pain medication. She rambled around in the draw beneath the papers, diapers and miscellaneous junk until she found a small, white bottle. She held it up to the side of her head and shook it until she heard something rattling inside. She lifted the lid off and emptied two white pills into her hand. Her eyes searched around the room for anything to drink, but all she saw were beer cans. She began shaking the cans until she found one with a trickle of beer remaining. She threw the pills in her mouth and washed them down before chunking it to across the room.

The sound of the can hitting the floor startled Tonya, who ran and jumped in the bed with her mother. She stared at her mother with worry and confusion.

"Mommy are you okay," she asked, tugging on her shirt.

Her mother looked at her, then turned back around without responding. Her body ached as she changed positions to try and get comfortable. No matter how she positioned herself, she just could not get comfortable.

After tossing and turning for about 30 minutes, she got up from the bed and made her way into the kitchen that looked like a tornado had passed through it. Dirty dishes filled the sink and cluttered the countertops. The trash was overflowing onto the floor and had a foul smell coming from it. It smelled like a mixture of old soiled diapers and rotten food. She made her way to the sink to find a clean glass to get a drink of water.

After drinking the water, she made her way into the living room and took a seat on the sofa in front of the television. As she sat there, looking at a blank screen, she realized something about her was different. She felt a little sick and drowsy. It was a little after noon on a Saturday afternoon and she had not eaten a thing. Normally, around this time of the day, she would have a strong appetite, especially after a night of drinking and smoking weed, but this morning, she had no appetite at all.

After grabbing some cookies from the table, Tonya joined her mother on the couch. She sat close to her mother and then, made her way into her lap. For a brief moment, Sharon held her daughter close before laying her down on the sofa. Within minutes, the toddler had fallen to sleep with cookies in hand.

While the child slept, Sharon made her way back to the kitchen and attempted to start cleaning. She was almost done with the kitchen when she heard the key in the front door. She knew it was Slick and wasn't sure if he was coming back to beat her again. She grabbed a knife from the kitchen drawer and prepared to defend herself. He walked into the kitchen as if he was in a rush. He sat down at the table without even looking in her direction. He abruptly got up from the table and grabbed a bag from the cabinet and sat back at the table. He then turned the paper bag upside down and shook it until several vials filled with a white-brown substance fell onto the table. His eyes widened with joy when he found his treasure. Sharon stared on in disbelief. She had never seen him with that much heroin before and she automatically knew that however he had gotten it was sure to bring trouble to their door step.

Her first thought was to ask where he had gotten the drugs, but before she could say a word, he began cooking up a spoonful. As she watched the flames of the lighter heat the spoon, she had a sudden itch and urge stirring in her veins. She was suddenly restless and couldn't seem to be still for too long. Inch by inch, she made her way over and joined Slick at the table, who was now drawing the liquid into the syringe.

She watched him intensely like a hungry child wanting a bite of her father's hamburger. As Slick examined the syringe, she held her arm out on the table in front of him. He looked up at her with partial grin on his face before tying her vein off. Her veins filled with blood jumped to the surface of her skin. Like a professional, he lined the needle above her skin and came in at an angle. There was a flash of blood in the tube and then it disappeared, along with the white mixture, into her arm. Lady Heroin now had her hooks deep in her flesh and gripped her tight. There was no escaping her now.

Later that evening, as she sat on the love seat watching television, there was a hard knock on the door. She got up and began walking toward the door before Slick came from the bedroom and motioned for her to move away from the door. He had a look of terror on his face as he stared at the door. The fear that covered his face was contagious. Sharon became afraid because she knew whoever was on the other side of the door was there because of the drugs they had enjoyed earlier that day.

The sound of the knocking woke the baby from her evening nap. She sat up on the couch and stared at the door where the knocks were coming from. Just as she climbed down off of the couch, the door exploded open from the impact of an 11 ½ boot that shattered the frame. Splinters from the door flew across the room in all directions.

A very large man appeared in the doorway. Sharon and Slick both backed up as far as they could until their backs made contact with the wall. The large man, followed by three others of similar build, stepped in through the broken door.

The man stood about 6'5 and looked like he weighed about 275 lbs. He had the look of death on his face as he scanned the room. Fists clenched, he walked into the middle of the room and paused before directing the other men to search the other rooms of the house. He watched Sharon and Slick closely without saying a single word. His demeanor said it all. The men reemerged from the rooms empty-handed.

"Where is my dope," he snarled, as he walked towards them.
"What dope, man? I don't have your dope."
"I'm going to ask you one more time. where's my shit?"

The men moved in closer to surround them. Sharon looked on in fear as Slick's knees started to tremble before he made a break for it. He took only two steps before being knocked off of his feet. His body hit the floor hard with a thud. Before he even had a chance to realize what had happened, they begin kicking and stomping him.

Tonya did her best to hide behind her mother's legs out of sight as the men viciously beat Slick within an inch of his life.

They then turned to Sharon who now had Tonya in her arms. She knew her only hope of not getting exactly what her husband had gotten was the child. She held her in her arms like a loving mother, hoping the sight of the child would cause the men to show her mercy.

It worked. The snarling beast calmed at the sight of the crying child who had her face buried in her mother's chest.

"Where's my dope?" the man asked.

Sharon knew that even the child would not save her if she didn't give them the drugs they came for. With her eyes, she directed them to the refrigerator where she thought Slick may have hid the drugs.

"Jackpot," one of the men said, as he pulled the brown paper bag from the freezer.

Before turning to walk out of the house, the lead man gave Slick one more hard kick to his head to make sure he got his message across. The tip of the steel toe boot connected with the side of his face square on his jaw, sending blood and broken teeth flying against the wall. His battered body lay motionless as the blood from his injuries stained the dirty carpet beneath him.

When the men left, Sharon put Tonya down on the floor and knelt down beside her wounded husband. She shook him in hopes of helping him regain consciousness, but he was unresponsive to her attempts. Unsure of what to do, she picked up the telephone and began calling the police, but then it hit her.

*How will I be able to explain what happened,* she wondered to herself. *I can't tell them about the drugs.*

She realized that if they found out that all of this was over drugs, they might search the house and find something else, which could mean jail for both of them. The thought of going to jail terrified her.

*If I tell the police about the men and they get arrested, they'll come back as soon as they bail out,* she thought.

Her thoughts were now rambling over the different courses of action she had to choose from. She decided to run down to the corner store to see if they had some smelling salt in stock. With blood on her shirt, she frantically ran into the store and scanned the shelves for the salt.

"Can I help you find something," the owner asked, as he watched her closely.

"Smelling salt, do you have any smelling salt?" she asked.

"Yes, aisles 3 on the middle right shelf near the nasal decongestion."

Sharon quickly paid for the salt with $1.75 in all coins and bolted out the door. Slick was still lying on the floor, unconscious, when she made it back to the house. She ripped the pack open and placed it under his nose. Suddenly, he began moving his head side to side slowly and then, his eyes opened. She continued to wave the smelling salt beneath his nose until he acted as if he could not bear the smell any longer. He was now fully alert, but unable to get up off of the floor.

Sharon placed his arm over her shoulder as Tonya sat on the couch watching them both closely.

"On the count of 3," she told him.

They simultaneously grunted as they struggled to lift him off the floor and on to the couch. He was in a lot of pain and she was still suffering from the pain he had inflicted upon her just the night before, but the love that she had for him gave her the strength to work through it. She worked feverously to make sure he was as comfortable as possible on the couch. She placed pillows under his head, feet and gave his a bag filled with ice to hold on the swollen areas of his body. For the next few days, she waited on him hand and foot, attending to his injuries. But, it wasn't long before neither of them could resist the urge of their new God, Heroin.

At first, Sharon only got the itch every few days, but week after week, she started to crave the drug more and more. After a long period without the drug, she would start to go through withdrawals and get dope sick.

It wasn't before long before she started stealing from the cash register at work to support her habit. Her paycheck just wasn't cutting it anymore and she needed other means to support her habit. Food and other items started coming up missing at the store and every time the store owner would question her about it, she would lie. One late afternoon, he called her into his office that was located back in the storage area. She stood in shock and shame as he showed her the video showing her stealing from the store.

"After all I've done for you, this is how you repay me," he said, shaking his head in disgust.

"I'm sorry, I am so sorry, it will never happen again, I promise," Sharon pleaded.

"You are right! It won't happen again. I want you to get your shit and get out of my store," he demanded, pointing at the exit.

"Please, don't fire me. I really need this job!"

"Get out," he shouted in a loud and thunderous voice.

She had never heard him use that tone before and the sound of his deep voice scared her. She quickly ran back to the front of the store and started collecting her belongs before running out of the store. She cried the entire way home.

Her hands trembled at the thought of telling Slick she had lost her job. She had no way of knowing, however, that that was exactly what he had hoped for when he initially introduced her to heroin. In his mind, the nickels and dimes she made at the store was nothing compared to what she could make by prostituting herself. He knew how men lusted over the very sight of her and, as long as he had her, he would always have a consistent way to get his true love, heroin.

Slick was sitting on the steps in front of the house when she made it home. He was fiddling with his hands when he noticed her walking up to the house.

"What are you doing home? Why aren't you at work?" he asked.

She began to walk slower as she got closer to where he was sitting. He stood up when she was within reach and took a step down off of the front steps.

"Woman, didn't you hear me ask you a question?" His voice was raised and took on a more serious tone.

"I, I, I…" she stuttered as if her words were stuck in her throat.

"Spit it out!" he yelled, as he took two more steps towards her.

"I got fired today for stealing that stuff from the store. He had me on tape and everything," she responded, now looking down at the ground.

Without warning, he slapped her hard across the face with an open hand. Blood flew from the corner of her mouth onto her shirt. Before she could raise her hand to her face, he slapped her again and again, each time hitting her harder. She tried to block his hands with her forearm, but he kicked her in the stomach, causing her to bend at the waist from the pain.

Passersby looked on, but kept their distance as he threw her to the ground and began to choke her. She cried and begged him to stop, but he continued until he was straddled on top of her. She gasped for air, but his hands squeezed tight, preventing air from entering her lungs. The choking caused her to spew blood onto his hands and face.

She was near unconsciousness when he released her bruised neck. Her eyes were wide as she placed her hands to her neck in relief. He had been completely silent and steel-faced during the initial part of the assault, but now his anger parted his lips and cut the air.

"You stupid, worthless bitch! How could you be so stupid to let him catch you?" he yelled.

"I'm sorry, I'm sorry," she cried.

Suddenly, he began to punch her with closed fists. Punch after punch rained down on her exposed face. The punches were so hard that they dazed her, causing her to drop her hands. She lay on the ground, defenseless, as the brutal assault continued.

Slick was nearly exhausted when he stopped hitting her. His knuckles were swollen and red from the contact against her bone and flesh. She was barely conscious and her face was bloody and swollen. A large gash ran from the corner of her eye to her cheek.

He rose and stood over her as she moaned in agonizing pain. It was his plan all along for her to quit or lose her job, but he took full advantage by using it as a reason to beat her nearly to death.

Neighbors and onlookers stood in the yards along the street and watched the entire time, but no one came to her rescue. No one intervened. No one called the police and no one whispered a word.

# Flesh of My Drug

Just as Slick had planned, Sharon was out of work and now had become so addicted to the drug that she began selling her body to support their habit. He may have been a junkie, but dumb was something he never was. The use of the heroin had slowed him down over the years and he knew it was just a matter of time before he needed a new hustle to continue to support his habit.

He saw how men looked at Sharon when she passed and he was banking that her pretty face and fine body would be beneficial in the long run. Men with money wouldn't hesitate to pay top dollar for a night of pleasure with a woman like her.

The first guy to proposition her was the very man who had beat Slick down only a few months ago. In the world of drugs, things like that quickly become a distant memory and the only thing that is relevant is what is right in front of you at that very moment and, at that moment, the itch for the drug was great. An episode of dope sickness had come down on them both and they were all out of money. They pretty much sold everything valuable in the house and stole from so many people that they were no longer welcome in the homes of most of the people they knew or were related to.

With the junkie monkey on her back, it didn't take much for Slick to convince her to take him up on his offer.

It was about 10 pm when he stopped by the house to find Sharon pacing the floor. She was nervous, but she was itching for it, bad.

The man, who she came to know as Justice, offered her four vials of smack in exchange for sex. People in the streets and involved in the drug trade called him Justice because he was infamously known for holding court in the streets and serving justice whenever he felt crossed or disrespected. He had scars on his hands and face, which served as testimony to anyone who may have had any doubt that he was battle-tested. He hardly ever smiled, but when he walked through the door, he had a huge one on his face.

The last time he was in their home, he was there on a business call. This time, however, it was strictly pleasure. He took a seat in the chair near the door and relaxed, his eyes following Sharon as she moved around the room. Despite the drug use, she still looked good and he liked what he saw.

She was dressed in a form-fitting party dress that accentuated her shape. She had put on a little makeup and a little perfume for the occasion. She was a certified junkie, but she cleaned up well. If it wasn't for her hair needing a perm, she would have almost looked like her old self.

Justice was not one for wasting time, so after getting a nice look at the merchandise, he exchanged a few words with Slick before tossing him a bag containing the four vials of heroin. He then picked Sharon up off of her feet like a husband does when taking his new bride over the threshold for the first time and carried her into the bedroom. Before she was out of sight, she looked back to see that Slick was so focused on the contents of the bag that he didn't bother looking up to see her being carried away by another man.

Sharon had never had sex for drugs before, but she expected it to be rough and it was just as she had expected. After carrying her in the room, he dropped her on the bed and directed her to undress. She undressed slowly as he stood by the bed watching. She tried to cover herself with the comforter that covered the bed, but he snatched it away and pulled her from the bed and forced her down on her knees. He unzipped his pants, exposing himself to her. After she went down on him, he pulled her up from the floor and bent her over the bed and began to have sex with her.

It was rough, unaffectionate and over in about 20 minutes, much to her relief. It was nothing like she had ever experienced, but it was over and she was eager to get to the drugs. Before he could zip up his pants, she was reaching for her clothes and running into the bathroom. She quickly got dressed and was about to walk out of the bathroom when she noticed her reflection in the mirror. She was ashamed of the person she saw and could only bear the sight of herself in the mirror for a few minutes. She shook her head in disgust, but the urge for a taste of the drug was too great for her to worry about that now.

She hurried out of the bathroom through the bedroom and down the hallway, passing the man along the way. Slick was already cooking up a spoonful of dope. She had just slept with another man, but neither of them gave it a thought as their eyes focused on the bubbles in the spoon.

They struggled in frustration to find a good vein to inject their dope, as all of the veins in their arms were too badly damaged from all the use. He told her to take off her shoes and she did. He found a nice vein running across the top of her foot and he inserted the tip of the needle. She felt the effects of the drugs instantly.

Slick took his shoe off and found his vein of his choice. It didn't take too long for him to feel the effects of the potent opiate.

Justice stood in the doorway leading into the living room, watching as they got high. He stood there until they were nearly in a stupor before walking toward the front door. Before he walked out of the door, he looked back to see Tonya now standing where he stood in the doorway. Her eyes were glued on him and a feeling of guilt came over him.

He turned around, walked back in and kneeled down in front of her. He looked her in her eyes before standing and leading her by the hand back into her bedroom. He picked her up and placed her in the bed and covered her beneath her blanket. For a second, he stood beside the bed, looking down upon her innocence.

He had a daughter of his own about her age and he knew that she had a rough life ahead of her, being the child of drug addicts. He, too, grew up as the child of an addict and knew firsthand, all too well, how hard of a life it had been. He was one of the most feared drug dealers in the city, but he had a soft spot in his heart for children. For a second, he thought about taking Tonya with him, but knew that would be a bad move. He kneeled down beside her bed and pulled the cover up to her chest.

"No matter what happens in your life, never stop believing in yourself," he said to her before standing up and walking out of the room. Before walking out of the front door of the house, he took one last look at Slick and Sharon, who were still zombie-like from their heroin. He shook his head in disappointment and walked out of the house, closing the door behind him.

During the early stages of her addiction, Sharon was able to maintain some form of her normal appearance. Once the word got out that she was now a drug whore, many of the men who had been pursuing her for years came a-looking.

It started with her accepting select men with money to come by the house, but the more the drug bug took hold of her, the more she roamed the streets in the wee hours of the morning, hoping to find someone willing to sleep with her for enough money to satisfy her ever-growing addiction. At first, she charged $250 for oral sex and $350 for oral sex and intercourse, but as her body started deteriorating from the frequent drug use, her stock decreased and so did her going rate.

The young lady that once upon a time drove men wild and made other women envious with her stunning looks and sassy ways was no more. She was now lost in a world where money and the next high were the only things that mattered. This was a cold, dark world where church wasn't even an afterthought and morals were nonexistent.

Sharon was now a woman of the night with one sole motivation in life: to chase the next high, by any means necessary. The former dream girl was now just a neighborhood junkie who traded sexual favors for drugs or money to get drugs.

She now lay with men who she had barely looked at or noticed in her better days. Just about every man to whom she had never given the time of day now took advantage of her addiction.

# A Dozen Dead Roses

# Death of an Angel

Tonya was only 13-years-old the morning she stepped out of the shower to find her stepfather standing in the bathroom, staring at her with that infamous sick grin across his face. She knew that very instant that she was in for a world of trouble. As her mother lay silently in her drug-induced sleep, Tonya's stepfather forced her naked body to the floor and took advantage of her.

"No," she begged, "please don't! I'm sorry, please let me go!" she pleaded with him. Despite her plea for mercy, he continued to force himself upon her.

"Mommy, mommy, please help me!" she cried out at the top of her lungs.

Her voice was quickly muffled by large, adult hands covering her mouth. She desperately tried to push him off of her, but the large man was too heavy. With one hand covering her mouth, he forced her legs apart and then forced himself inside of her.

The sharp pain from the initial penetration was so intense; it nearly caused her pass out.

"Keep your ass still," he demanded, as she squirmed to try and escape the pain of her attacker.

As he moved his hand from over her mouth to try and kiss her, she bit down on his top lip so hard that it drew blood.

"Agh, you stupid bitch!" he yelled.

Angered by her defiance, he snatched her head up from the floor by her hair and smashed it back down with enough force that it knocked her unconscious. As she lay silent and motionless, he continued to have his way with her.

Nearly an hour later, she awoke, still lying on the cold, damp floor, bleeding from between her legs and the back of her head. She struggled to pull herself up from the blood-covered floor and stumbled into her mother's room, in hopes of protection. There was none.

Tonya's mother lay still and motionless as Tonya struggled to awaken her. As the pain gripped her stomach, Tonya fell to the floor in exhaustion and covered herself in tears.

The following days, she tried to tell her mother about what her stepfather had done, but her mother only responded with degrading insults.

"You are nothing but a little whore. I see how you parade around in front of him, trying to get his attention. You better not tell anyone; if you do, Social Services will put your little hot ass in a foster home."

Her body was still hurting from the trauma, but her soul was now dying inside of her as she stood paralyzed in a trance.

The following week, she came up with a plan to run away from home. She had been saving change she found around the house and stealing from her parents, and she now had about $220. Her plan was to sneak out in the middle of the night with as much food and water as she could carry and find her long-lost father.

Her mother had tried her best to convince her over the years that her father didn't want her and had abandoned them before she was born. Tonya had heard her mother say this a million times, but she never truly believed it. She often imagined that her father would someday show up and take her away to his big house where she would live with him forever.

She waited until everyone was fast asleep and went into the kitchen, where she had hidden a bag of all the food she could scavenge up the week leading up to her planned escape. It was about 3 in the morning when she made her way out of the back door and around the house to the sidewalk. She ran as fast as her legs could carry her as she made her way to the metro bus stop. Her heart was pounding in her chest, but there was no turning back now.

Fear of the unknown gripped her at every dark alleyway she crossed and at every noise she heard. Her hands were trembling, but she pushed on toward the bus stop. When she arrived at the bus stop, she scanned the area for danger before checking the bus schedule. Just as she started scanning the schedule, the bus turned the corner and pulled up directly in front of her. She hurried onto the bus and dropped a token in the pay slot.

"Little girl, what are you doing out this time of the night?" the bus driver asked with irritation in his voice. "Does your mother know where you are at?"

"Yes, sir," she responded before taking her seat.

The driver turned around while shaking his head in disgust without saying another word and guided the bus away from the curb. After several more stops, the driver turned and told her that this was the last stop. She grabbed her things and hurried off of the bus and took a seat along the curb. It dawned on her that she really didn't have anywhere to go and didn't even know where to start looking for her father. She had never even seen as much as a picture of him and wouldn't know what he looked like if he walked right up to her.

Frustrated, she got up from the curb and began to walk up the block toward the lights coming from the corner store. As she got closer, she noticed several men gathered around the store laughing and talking as if they were having the time of their lives. They all seemed drunk and she knew it wouldn't be good if they saw her all alone at that time of the night.

She hesitated for a minute and waited for an opportunity to sneak by unnoticed. When it appeared that the men were distracted by their conversation, she made a dash for it. Running at full speed with bags in hand, she made her way around the corner. Out of breath and out of danger for the moment, she stopped to catch her breath and gather her thoughts. After catching her breath, she started walking, without any clear direction where she was headed.

Her plan now was just to keep walking until she could figure out her next move. After about an hour of walking, an old model brown car with dark tinted windows slowed down as it passed her. She could see the shape of a man behind the tint, but she was not able to see his face. She continued walking as the car turned the corner, but suddenly she noticed the car turning around and coming in her direction.

*Maybe he is lost*, she thought to herself, as she started back walking. As the car crept past her again, the driver's side window slowly came down and she could now see a dirty-looking man staring at her as the car stopped. He stuck his arm out of the window and motioned for her to come to the car. Tonya ignored his gesture and began walking fast in the opposite direction. The man made another U-turn in the middle of the avenue and pulled up behind her. In a panic, she dropped all of her belongings and took off in a full sprint.

She heard the car door slam behind her and she knew that he was on foot after her. She looked back over her shoulder to see the man running after her.

"Somebody help me! Please help me!" she screamed at the top of her lungs as she ran across the street.

She could now hear his footsteps getting closer to her as she neared the corner. At the corner, she realized she was back at the very corner store with the men standing out front, but before she could take another step, the man grabbed her from behind, placing his hand over her mouth to prevent her from screaming. He then lifted her off of her feet and started carrying her back towards the direction of his car in a hurry. Her little legs kicked frantically to no avail. Beneath his hands, her screams for help turned to cries for mercy.

Only a few feet from his car, he could hear voices coming up from behind him. He turned to see that the men from the store were running in his direction.

"Hey! Hey! What are you doing?" they yelled from a distance.

This caused the man to start walking faster toward his car. He opened the door and tried to force Tonya inside. She managed to grab the side of the door, preventing him from pushing her completely inside the car. He tried to pry her fingers off the door frame, but the men were coming up on them fast. Tonya was now hanging on for dear life, for she knew if he got her in the car, she would never be seen again.

"Help me!" she screamed out to the men.

The men were only 50 yards away when the strange man released her and ran around to the driver side of his car. She was hanging halfway out of the car when the man sped away from the curb. The swerving motion of the car threw her into the street.

One of the men rushed to her side and quickly lifted her up into his arms and carried her out of the street.

"Little girl, are you okay?" he asked with concern in his voice.

Tonya was still screaming for help. The fall from the car had shaken her up, but she was uninjured. Still in shock from the near abduction, she suddenly began to fight to get away from the men who were now standing over her.

"Leave me alone!" she yelled as she tried to break through their circle.

"Calm down, little lady, we are only trying to help you," one of the men said, in a calm voice. "You are safe now."

In all the commotion, she failed to realize that one of the men was friends with her stepfather. In that same very instance, he too realized who she was.

"Man, that's Sharon's little girl!" he yelled to the other men.

"Sharon?" another man asked, as if he didn't know who the other man was talking about.

"Yeah, Sharon! Slick's ole lady."

"Oh, yeah, Sharon that lives in the green house on 4th street," another man said.

"Little girl, what are you doing out here this time of the night?" the man holding her asked.

Before she could answer, another man interrupted, "Does your mother know that you are out here?"

She stared down at the ground and said nothing. The man leaned over and told her to stand up, which she did. Her first thought was to run away from the group of men, but the fear of the other man who had tried to kidnap her coming back made her stay in place.

"We should take her home," one of the men said.

"Yeah, let's do that," another agreed.

As they walked down the street toward the bus stop, Tonya reluctantly dragged along with them. She knew she would be in a lot of trouble for trying to run away, but there was nothing she could do about it at this point. The large city bus pulled up to the stop and all of the men got on behind her and they all sat in the back of the bus. For the first few minutes, no one said anything until one of them, who seemed to be the elder of the group, spoke.

"Young lady, something really bad could have happened to you if we wouldn't have come along," he said. "There are some crazy people out here this time of the night who would love nothing more than to get their filthy hands on a little girl like you."

The other men nodded their heads in agreement.

"Where were you going, anyway?" one asked.

She sat silent and did not even acknowledge the question. Her mind was now completely on the trouble that awaited her at home.

Frustrated from the lack of response from her, the man asked, "Little girl, don't you hear me talking to you?"

She didn't even look in his direction or act as if she heard the question. She stared straight out of the bus window. At every stop, her heart rate increased because she knew each stop meant she was closer to home, a place she dreaded going to.

When the bus pulled up to their stop, all of the men got off, but Tonya refused to leave her seat. She held on tight to the pole that was next to her seat. The men looked back at her with puzzled, concerned looks on their faces. The bus driver stared impatiently in the rearview mirror, as if to say, "Hurry up and get on or off my bus."

Before he could close the door, one of the men jumped back on the bus and grabbed her by the arm and literally pulled her off of the bus. She held onto the pole as long and as hard as she could, but the man was just too strong. His strength over-powered hers. She stood there with tears in her eyes as she watched the bus pull away from the stop.

"Girl, what is wrong with you," the man screamed, as he turned her to face him. "Are you crazy or something?"

"I think something is wrong with her, man, she may be a little touched or something," another said.

"Your mother must have been high as hell when she had you," another chimed in.

"Leave that child alone," the oldest of the men said to the rest of the men. "Don't you see the child is scared? Baby, it's going to be okay, you are almost home with your mother."

Little did he know, the thought of her being almost back home was what had her scared to death. He held her hand as he guided her up the walkway to the front door. The other men followed behind them, but stopped short of the steps leading up to the porch that surrounded the front part of the house.

Tonya's heart was racing as the man hit the door with 3 hard knocks. The house was as quiet as a mouse, but the curtain in the widow near the front door moved slightly to the side just enough for someone to peek out of it without being noticed. In the life her parents lived, one could never be certain who would be coming looking for them or what their intentions were. They were always on edge and paranoid.

Tonya, who had seen both of her parents look out the window in that manner every time someone knocked on the door, knew exactly where to look. She could see her stepfather's eyes scanning from the man on the porch to the men standing at the bottom of the steps.

The window curtain closed slowly to avoid being noticed. The man knocked on the door several more times, but this time he hit the door much harder, creating a booming sound from the impact of his knuckles to the wooden door.

Just as the man turn to say something to the other men, he noticed a skinny figure hurrying up the side walk toward the house. It was Sharon and the sight of the men at the door automatically put a smile on her face. The sight of men at her house that time of the night usually meant money or drugs. Either was fine with her. She tried to put on her sexy walk as she made her way up the walkway to where the men were standing.

They all looked at her like a pack of wolves waiting to attack their prey. The heroin had done a lot of damage to her appearance, but the intoxicated men didn't really care at that time of the night.

Sharon was so focused on the men that she didn't notice Tonya standing on the porch, partially hidden behind the man.

"You boys come to party?" she asked in a flirtatious voice. "I hope y'all got some money."

"No, we are not here for that." one of the men interrupted. "We found your daughter over by the liquor store on Market Blvd. There was some crazy fool trying to kidnap her or something, but we chased him off."

"We are just bringing her home. You know a little girl shouldn't be out at this time of the night walking the streets, Sharon," another man on the porch said, with irritation in his voice.

"Looks like she was trying to run away," one of them men said, as he extended his arm to hand her the book bag that contained the items Tonya has packed. "Something bad could have happened to her."

Sharon looked up at the man and, for the first time, noticed Tonya standing next to him. Just then, the front door flew open and Slick stepped out on to the porch. He had been standing behind the door, listening the entire time. He roughly grabbed the child by her arm and pulled her away from the man.

"Get your ass in the house," he shouted, as he shoved her toward the open door.

The force caused her to stumble and fall just inside of the door, but as soon as she hit the floor, she jumped up and ran as fast as she could to her room.

"Hey man! Don't do that child like that," one of the men standing at the bottom of the steps yelled at Slick, as he took a step up toward the porch.

His face was covered with anger and the man now stared hard at Slick with a clinched fist.

"I don't want no problem," Slick responded. "Now, get off my property before I call the police."

As he turned to walk back into the house, Sharon hurried up the steps and followed him into the house. The door slammed behind her and the men walked away, talking amongst themselves about what had just happened.

Inside the house, Tonya hid under her bed, terrified. She could hear her stepfather walking through the house, making a lot of noise like he was looking for something.

Without warning, he burst through her bedroom door.

"Where are you?" he yelled, as he searched the room for her.

He looked in the closet first before finding her under the bed.

"Come from under there!" he yelled, as he pushed the bed back against the wall.

As the child curled up into a ball on the floor and buried her face in her hands, he stood towering above her with an extension cord wrapped partially with duct tape in his hand.

"You want to run away," he shouted down to her. "Stupid little bitch, I'm going to show you who is boss around here!"

He raised his arm up over his shoulder, bringing his hand as far as he could until the end of the extension cord was nearly at his lower back and brought it forward in a whipping motion, bringing the weapon down across her back. The sound of the cord tearing and ripping her flesh through her shirt echoed off of the bedroom walls. A large welt instantly appeared across her back where the cord made contact.

She yelled out in sheer pain and tried to scoot out of the way of danger. The next lash was across her arm that she held up to protect herself. She crawled back under the bed as fast as she could and moved as far as she could away from the side he was standing on.

He pulled the bed back to the middle of the room, but she moved quickly in the direction the bed moved, keeping herself covered.

In frustration, he walked out of the room and again, she heard him rambling for something through the house. She remained under the bed, crying and trembling. The pain from the welt ached, but she ignored it and kept her focus on the doorway. She thought, for a second, that maybe it was over, but didn't want to take the chance of leaving the only shelter that protected her.

His dirty boots appeared in the doorway and again, he began pushing and pulling the bed across the wooden floor, trying to catch her, but she was able to stay with the bed and out of his reach.

He kneeled down and attempted to crawl under the bed after her, but she escaped to the other side and when he came from under the bed, she crawled back under it. The cat and mouse game continued for several more minutes, which enraged him. He cursed and demanded for her to come from beneath the bed, but she refused and continued to evade him in defiance.

He left the room infuriated and slammed the door shut behind him.

"I'll get you, you little bitch!" he shouted back at her as he marched down the hallway and out of the house. She relaxed a little when she heard the front door to the house slam.

For the next two hours, she stayed under the bed and on guard. The sun was now coming up and the long night of sleeplessness was wearing on her. Her tired, little mind began to drift and before long, she was fast asleep beneath the bed.

She had been asleep for about an hour when the sound of the legs of the bed scraping across the floor awakened her. She tried to quickly get back under the bed, but Slick placed his foot on her neck and pressed in down on the floor.

"No!" She screamed while kicking.

He snatched her up from the floor. She struggled to free herself as he dragged her into the living room and tied her to the wooden pillar that divided the living room from the dining area. He tied her standing with her face against the beam and arms around it, leaving her back facing him. She frantically scanned the room for her mother, but she had already left the house again.

She begged and pleaded with him for mercy to no avail and her attempts to free her hands were futile. She was helpless and at his mercy as he stared at her like a crazed, wild beast. He picked up the whip he had made from the extension cord and duct tape and began to savagely beat her across her back. The strike of the cord tore open her shirt and ripped gashes in her skin, drawing blood with each lash. She tried to move away from the whip by turning around the pole but he continued to whip her indiscriminately all over her body, arms, and legs. He continued to beat her until he was nearly exhausted and foaming at the mouth.

Her beaten body hung limp against the beam. When he was done beating her, he dragged her into the darkened hallway closet and locked her inside. She lay on the floor, curled in a ball, whimpering in pain and anguish from the stinging wounds that covered her body. Her shirt was torn and stained with blood from the savage beating at the hands of her stepfather, but her spirit wasn't unbroken.

After several hours of lying there, she managed to lift herself up into a sitting position. The only light she had was coming from the crack that ran beneath the door. The house was now completely quiet and the only sound that could be heard was the dripping faucet in the bathroom.

The closet had been completely emptied out and all that was left inside was a bucket that sat in the corner of the cramped space. The night had come and gone and when the morning arrived, she remained trapped in the closet. She could barely move around in the small closet and the smell of her own urine and feces grew worse by the hour. Her body grew weak from hunger and the lack of water. It was a dark and lonely place inside the closet, but she was able to find peace in the fact that at least she was safe, for the time being. No one was in the house, so she didn't have to worry about anyone bothering her in the night as she slept.

It had nearly been two days since she had been beaten and locked in the closet when she heard the front door open and footsteps in the house. She wasn't sure who it was who had entered the house, so she kept quiet to avoid being detected. The clinging of metal made her nervous. She started to wonder if her stepfather had gone and found something worse with which to beat her. As the footsteps neared the door, she braced herself for the worst.

The door opened and her stepfather stood there, looking as if he was fresh off of a two-day drug binge. He reached in and dragged her from the closet by her bound hands.

"I brought you a present," he said, as he dragged her down the hallway toward her bedroom. He released her and closed the door once he had her inside.

Inside the room was a rusted dog cage that looked like something someone had thrown out beside the road. There was a bucket filled halfway with water and old bag of Purina puppy chow inside the cage. He walked over to it and opened the small door and told her to get in. She sat silently, staring at the cage, but didn't move. He reached over on the dresser and grabbed the taped extension cord that he had beaten her with before and showed it to her in a threatening gesture. Reluctant-ly, she made her way over the cage and climbed inside. He placed a small padlock on the door and placed the key on the dresser. Before walking out of the room, he kneeled down in front of the cage and said, "Since you want to run away from home like a dog, I'm going to treat you like a dog."

Tonya began to cry and beg as she watched him walk away and close the bedroom door behind him.

"Please, let me out," she begged. "I won't run away again, I promise. Please, just let me out!"

Her cries fell on deaf ears and once again, she was left in the house alone. After about an hour, she managed to stop crying and it was then that she realized that she had not eaten since being locked in the closet. She stared at the dog food that he had left for her and just couldn't bring herself to eat it.

As the day blended into the night, the old house grew dark and the silence was eerie. All that could be heard was the sound of mice scurrying about in search of food and the dripping faucet in the back room. She tried her best to get comfortable in the wiry metal on which she sat and leaned. It was a far stretch from the softness of the worn out mattress on her bed. She wanted to stretch her leg out so badly, but the cage was just too small. Occasionally, she would doze off, but her hunger pangs would always wake her up.

She now had a constant hunger headache and her body was getting weaker from the starvation, but it wasn't until about 6 the next morning when she finally broke down.

A Dozen Dead Roses

She slowly opened up the bag and reluctantly looked inside. The aroma of the stale-smelling contents was not appetizing, but she had to eat. She reached in, picked two bites from the bag and held her breath before placing them in her mouth. Just as she had expected, it tasted like cardboard, but she continued to chew. She swallowed the two bites, then scooped up a handful from the bag and threw it in her mouth.

She leaned over and took a sip of water from the bucket before taking another helping from the bag. After about four handfuls, she closed the bag and placed it behind her back to try and give herself some relief from the metal cage.

Around noon that day, she awakened to the sound of someone moving around in the front part of the house. From the sound of it, there was another man in the house having a conversation with her mother and Slick. After they finished talking, she could hear them walking into the bedroom next to hers and door closing. She had heard this many times before during the night, so she placed her fingers in her ears to try and block out the sound. The moans started low, but got louder as the headboard began to bang harder and faster against the wall that separated the rooms. She closed her eyes tight and tried to imagine being somewhere else, but the sound of her bedroom door opening quickly snapped her back to reality.

She opened her eyes to find Slick's evil eyes zoomed in on her through the cracked door. He watched her like animal watches its prey before killing it. The door closed, but she knew he would be back. She was so focused on the door that she didn't even realize that the noise from the other room had stopped.

Again, she could hear heavy footsteps in the hallway heading toward the front door. She thought to scream out for help, but was more afraid of what would happen if she did, so she kept her mouth closed. The sound of the front door closing meant once again, she would be home alone with two monsters. She knew after they got high, her nightmare would begin, so she tried to prepare herself for what was to come.

About two hours after hearing the john leave, her bedroom door opened again and her stepfather stepped inside with an evil grin on his face. He grabbed the extension cord from the dresser before opening up the cage door. He told her to get out and forced her to undress and lay on the bed.

As she lay naked across the bed, he struck her violently across her bare back with the weapon and warned her not to move.

"That's just a taste of what I'll give you if you try to resist," he snarled, as he climbed on top of her.

## A Dozen Dead Roses

Her eyes watered with tears of pain as he raped her again while her mother slept in a drug-induced high. As he raped her, all she could think was that she hadn't seen her mother in three days.

# Motherly Love

Over the next couple of years, Tonya's stepfather continued to sexually abuse her without any objections from her mother. Her mother was madly addicted to heroin and was not about to lose the provider of what she loved more than anything in the world.

Around age 14, Tonya's mother and stepfather started forcing her to sleep with different neighborhood drug dealers for drugs. By age 15, she became pregnant with her first child. Unsure of who the father was, her first thought was to have an abortion but gave up on that thought when she found out how much it would cost.

Despite her being pregnant, her stepfather continued to molest her and trade her for drugs when the junkie monkey was on his back.

Over and over, she thought about killing herself, but couldn't bring herself to do it until one day, she just couldn't take any more.

She was tired from being up so late the night before when one of the regular Johns stopped by to be serviced. This particular John was a corrupt police officer who everyone knew as Franklin. He was infamously known throughout the neighborhood for planting drugs on people and then, threatening them with jail time to get them to do his bidding.

He had arrested Slick and Sharon a few months back for illegal drug possession and, in order to stay out of jail, Slick offered up Tonya. Slick knew that Franklin had a reputation for being very fond of young girls and boys and tonight, he was coming by for one of his payments for his kindness, as he liked to call it.

Just like the time before, he directed her to perform oral sex on him and then, he instructed her to lie back on the bed as he climbed on top of her. She lay in her bed, feeling sick to her stomach as the large man had his way with her.

She closed her eyes and tried to block out the moment from her mind like always, but she was unable to ignore the foul stench of the hairy, obese man. She wanted to cry, but there were no more tears left in her eyes.

She began to pray and ask God to take her. At that very moment, she had given up her will to live and decided that night would be her last night in this cruel world.

While the john was in the bathroom, cleaning himself up, Tonya took his police revolver from the holster and aimed it at her face. The gun exploded and jolted her across the room. When she awoke, she found herself in a hospital bed, surrounded by flowers and balloons bought by the hospital staff. Due to her shaking hands and closed eyes, her aim was poor causing the bullet to strike her in the upper-chest, missing any vital organs.

When she realized she was not dead, she broke down crying at the thought of her failure. *God must truly hate me to leave me in this world*, she thought to herself.

A knock on the door broke her thoughts, as a woman carrying an infant walked in the room. She had almost forgotten she was pregnant until she saw the baby

"Is that my baby?" she asked, before the woman could speak.

"Yes, this is your little girl. Would you like to hold her?" the nurse asked her, with a bright smile on her face.

She felt dirty and unworthy of such a beautiful child and refused to hold her own daughter.

"No! Get that thing out of here," she yelled at the nurse.

Shocked, the nurse quietly left the room. Moments later, a doctor entered the room, followed by another nurse.

"Good morning," he said, with a polite tone. "That is a pretty bad wound you have there."

She sat silently as the doctor began to talk to her about the extent of her injury that was a result of her accidental shooting and the birth of her premature baby.

Before she could tell the doctor the shooting was not an accident, her stepfather and mother walked into the room. The sight of them both sickened her and brought chills of fear over her body. For the first time in her young life, she watched her parents act like normal, loving, caring people, but she knew it was all just an act.

Over the next couple of months while Tonya was recovering, the nurse continually brought little Raven, her unwanted daughter, in to visit her.

It took about a month of persistence of trying before the sight of the beautiful, brown-eyed baby broke her down. She had never known love before, but she knew that she loved Raven very deeply.

She had decided to name her Raven because, as a small child, she always wished she could fly away like the birds in the sky and escape. Exactly four months after the shooting, she and Raven were released from the hospital with a good bill of health. For the first six months, back at home, she mostly stayed locked in her room with her bundle of joy. But one evening, while in the kitchen, cleaning out Raven's baby bottle, she heard baby cries coming from her bedroom.

When she rushed back to the room, she found her stepfather standing over Raven with that same sick grin on his face. She made a quick attempt to grab Raven from the bed, but before she could, he reached down and grabbed the child.

The sight of Raven in her stepfather's arms took the breath out of her. Her first thought was to cry, but her motherly instincts kicked in and she immediately charged him, swinging with all her might. She landed two hard blows to the side of his face before he knocked her to the floor with a strong backhand. She sprang from the floor unfazed by the blow to her head and charged in again, kicking and swinging wildly, nearly hitting Raven. One wild swing struck home and drew blood from his mouth. Enraged, he dropped Raven to the floor and swung with all his might, striking her in her right eye and sending her crashing to the floor. Her eye began swelling instantly from the violent punch.

A throbbing sensation rushed through her head as she attempted to lift her body from the floor, preparing to attack again. Before she could move, the sight of her stepfather's hands around Raven's neck stopped her in her tracks.

"Please don't hurt her," she begged.

"I will break this little bitch's neck if you don't start acting right around here," he threatened. "Since you had been up at that hospital around them uppity niggas and white folks, you think you're better than somebody."

The will to fight had left her and she knew she had to submit for the safety of her daughter. Tears rolled down her face as she started to undress to his delight. As he grunted and humped on top of her, she laid there stone-faced and emotionless.

Her only thoughts were of Raven. She no longer loved herself, but her love for Raven was the only thing keeping her alive. She knew that if she killed herself, Raven would be left in this world to suffer the same or worse fate at the hands of her parents.

Over the next couple of years, the abuse continued and continually increased as her little girl body began to grow into that of a woman's.

Without access to any kind of birth control, it wasn't long before she became pregnant again. Just like the time before, she had no clue who the father could have been. There were so many different johns coming in and out of the house to see her. That, coupled with the fact that her stepfather would rape her almost any time he got the urge, meant that it was anyone's guess as to who the father of the child could be.

She first started experiencing morning sickness. After about two months, she was showing signs of a baby bump. Her mother, who was now hardly ever around, caught notice of it one afternoon before leaving the house.

Without warning or provocation, she grabbed Tonya.

"Bitch, I know you are not pregnant again." We barely can feed the mouths we already got living in this house. I don't know what you are going to do, but ain't another baby coming up in this house."

Slick, who was out on the porch, overheard the conversation and stormed into the house with his fist balled.

"Baby?-Baby? You stupid bitch," he said, as he shook his head from side to side in disbelief. "I can't believe you let somebody knock you up again!"

He looked at her for a moment with such venom that she drew back away from him.

"Hell no"! There won't be any more babies coming out of your dirty ass! You'd better fix it before I do," he yelled at the top of his lungs while pounding his right fist in the palm of his left hand.

He had beaten her many times before and the sight of him terrified her. She knew she had to do something, but didn't know what do. Somehow, she had to get rid of the baby before Slick tried to beat it out of her.

That night, while lying in bed with Raven, she remembered how she had rejected her at first, but eventually fell in love with her. Despite how she came into this world, Raven was her daughter and she loved her more than anything else in the world, including herself. She stroked her daughter's face as she slept peacefully. The moonlight peeking through the window blinds shined down on her, making it look as if she was under a spotlight.

Tonya saw this as a sign from God and realized, at the very moment, that there was no way she could kill the child that was growing inside of her. She would rather die than to kill her child. She began to smile at the thought of possibility of having a boy and Raven having a little brother to play with.

As the weeks and month went by, her stomach grew bigger. Unlike before, the johns stopped coming by as much as they once did. The large, pregnant teenage girl was no longer as attractive as she once had been.

When the money or drugs weren't coming in as they used to, she knew it was just a matter of time before the beating at the hands of her stepfather would began.

Sometimes the physical abuse was something as simple as a slap across the face and there were times when there were all-out assaults.

It was around midday and she had just finished changing Raven and putting her down for a nap. As soon as the baby was fast asleep, she took that opportunity to climb into the bed beside her to get in a little nap of her own. The cool breeze from the window and the sound of the music coming from the radio created a very relaxing atmosphere and, in no time, she was fast asleep.

A few minutes into her nap, she drifted off into a dream of her playing in a park with Raven and a little boy who looked like her. They were so happy as they played peek-a-boo between taking bites of the snacks they had in the picnic basket.

Abruptly, her dream was interrupted by a tug on her leg. She opened her eyes to find Slick standing at the foot of the bed holding onto her ankles. She tried to grab hold of the bed, but it was too late. When he pulled again, her entire body lifted from the bed and landed hard on the floor. Her sternum hit the floor with thud, nearly knocking the wind from her body.

She tried to crawl under the bed for shelter, but he was still pulling hard on her legs. As she held onto the bottom of the brown wooden bedpost for dear life, she could smell the stench of Pine-Sol. Her hands were growing weak and slipping from the post. She quickly tried to adjust to get a better grip, but her sweaty hands slipped off, allowing him to pull her into the bathroom by her feet.

Awaiting them in the bathroom was her mother with a bottle of Pine-Sol and some pills. Tonya struggled to free herself from Slick's grip and escaped out the door, but her hopes were dimmed when her mother closed the door and locked it. Raven, who had been awakened by the struggle, was now in the bedroom alone, crying at the top of her lungs. Both mother and daughter's screams cut like a razor's edge through the house.

Unfazed by the screams and pleas for mercy, Slick released her and told her to stand up. She stood with tears pouring from her eyes and her back against the wall in shear fright, covering her face.

"Please, I'm sorry," she pleaded, without knowing what she had done.

"Give it to her," he directed.

Sharon, who was blocking Tonya's only possible route of escape, held a bottle of Tamoxifen in one hand and a glass filled with a colored liquid in the other. She handed Tonya the glass and told her to drink it. Before even putting the cup up to her mouth, she could smell the strong scent of Pine-Sol coming from the cup, and inside the cup she noticed what look-liked crushed pills floating around. She shook her head in refusal and tried to hand the glass back to her mother.

"Bitch, I told you there will not be another baby coming out of you! Now, drink the damn water," he demanded.

"I don't want to kill my baby. Please don't make me do it. I will do anything. Please, please don't," she begged.

Slick grabbed her and threw her to the floor. He straddled her legs and pinned her arms above her head.

"Nooo!" she screamed at the top of her lungs, as she struggled to free herself.

He continued to hold her down as her mother attempted to force the bleach down her mouth. The heavy flow of liquid filled her mouth and nose, making her feel as if she was drowning. She tossed her head from side to side to prevent the bleach from getting in her mouth.

"Hold her mouth open," her mother instructed Slick.

Wave after wave of poison liquid rushed down her throat like a raging river of death, entering her stomach and lungs. She gagged violently trying to force the fluids from her body, causing her to vomit all over the bathroom floor and on Slick. This, of course, angered him.

He rose from the floor and proceeded to kick her repeatedly in her swollen stomach.

"Dumb-bitch!" he shouted.

Tonya curled in the fetal position and wrapped her arms around her belly to protect her unborn.

The onslaught continued until he was nearly out of breath. He dropped back down to the floor and attempted to roll her over. In deep pain, she held her body rigid and tight, preventing him from being able to pin her down. He pulled hard to pry her arms away from her midsection, but she held her hands together tightly until she couldn't hold them any longer.

Her hands parted and he was able to roll her onto her back. He straddled her legs again and her mother grabbed her chin to hold her head in place. Again, she tried to force the bleach down Tonya's throat.

The horrible taste of the mixture of Pine-Sol and abortion drug burned the inside of her mouth and nostrils burned from the fumes. Gulp after gulp, she was forced to swallow nearly half of the glass of liquid.

After feeling satisfied that their work was done, he released her and they walked out of the bathroom, leaving her on the floor. Pain gripped her stomach as she curled into a ball against the bathtub. Blood stained her pants between her legs and she moaned in agonizing pain on the same damp floor where she was raped by her stepfather.

It wasn't until a week later that she was able to go to the hospital to be seen. Since the attack, she had fallen into a state of depression. Just as she had expected, the doctor informed her that she had had a miscarriage and required a medical procedure to remove the dead fetus from her womb.

Even though she already knew that she had lost the child, it hurt to hear the doctor's words. She had been praying that somehow, the child would survive, but her doctor confirmed her fears. The child had been poisoned and beaten to death inside of her.

# A Supreme Summer

It was the summer of her 17th birthday when she met Malik Robertson, better known around the neighborhood as Supreme. He was one of the most popular guys around town and the most recruited star athlete in the Southeast. He had the kind of personality that seem to make people gravitate towards him. He played basketball, soccer and football for the local high school and all of the top colleges were doing everything they could to convince him to come to their respective schools.

Almost weekly, a scout from one of the schools or a professional baseball team were at his parents' home, most of the time with gifts in hand, hoping to sway them into allowing their son to play for their team. Almost instantly after meeting him, the scouts fell in love with his maturity, confidence and mannerisms. He was well-raised and a very respectable young man who just had a strong presence about him wherever he went. He stood about 5'10" with an athletic build, broad shoulders and the facial features of his father.

His father was retired military, so at a very early age, he was taught to take pride in his appearance and to keep himself in fighting shape. He was well-known throughout the neighborhood for running almost everywhere he went. When he didn't have anywhere to go, he could be found running through the neighborhoods and parks around the city, just for fun.

Every mile or so, he would find a clear spot of grass and stop to do push-ups and sit-ups, which helped him build and maintain a lean, muscular physique.

There was just something about Supreme that people just couldn't get enough of. This included women and girls of all ages. They were just heads over heels for him, but surprisingly to many, he had a crush on Tonya. He would always go out of his way to speak to her every chance he got, but she would always respond with a very dry and disinterested look.

The abusive mistreatment at the hands of her stepfather had taken a toll on her and she became very mean and cold toward men and, in her eyes, Supreme was no different.

Despite not being able to wear the latest in fashion or to get her hair done up in the trendy hair-dos, Tonya's beauty was undeniable. She had the looks of her father and the body of her mother. Her hair, when unwrapped, hung down to the small of her back. Her dimples were deep and complemented her beautiful smile.

What Supreme liked most about her was that she was smart and that she kept to herself. During his runs through the parks, he would occasionally come across her sitting beneath a tree reading a book. He would always try to get her attention as he ran by, but she would only look up long enough to roll her eyes and look back down at the book. She was different than all the other girls around his age and this attracted him even more. She was never at any of his games and she never went out of her way to get his attention like the other girls around his age. She was quiet and the other girls always seemed to be talking. Tonya never seemed to care about designer clothes and that's all the other girls seemed to care about.

The fondness that Supreme had for her did not come without a price. All of the girls who liked Supreme hated her and took every opportunity they could to call her a crack whore with a bastard child. When she walked by, they would make it their business to try and pick a fight with her by blocking her path. When they caught her in the bathroom alone, they would gang up and corner her while pulling on her clothes and hair.

There was one girl in particular who disliked Tonya the most. Angela Keys was one of the most popular girls in school. She came from an upper-middle class family that was able to afford her the comforts of life, such as designer clothes, jewelry, perfume and just about any other thing her heart desired. Angela had held a crush on Supreme since they were in elementary school and, for years, told her friends that he would one day be her husband.

Despite her persistent attempts to woo him, he hardly paid her any attention after their brief courtship. During their short-lived relationship, he became quickly irritated by her constant shallow and vain conversation. When he would attempt to discuss a serious topic, she would always change the subject to something he had absolutely no interest in.

Angela was extremely cruel to Tonya and Tonya tried her hardest to never let her see her cry. But, beneath the tough exterior, Angela's words pierced her feelings like a thrown spear.

She spent many days in the bathroom stalls, crying her eyes out as a result of the humiliation. She hated going to school and going to the bathroom while at school even more. She would try as hard as she could to hold it until school let out, but there were days that she just couldn't.

On one particular day after Spring Break, Angela and her crew followed Tonya to the bathroom. While two of the girls held her and the other blocked the door so no one could get in, Angela took out a pair of scissors and started cutting out large locks of her hair. She fought as hard as she could to free herself, but the two large girls held her in place long enough for a few inches of her hair to be cut out. Before leaving the bathroom, the girls took turns punching her. To add insult to injury, Angela, the meanest of them all, slapped her as hard as she could across the face before spitting on her. The bullying at the hands of the girls had almost become a routine thing for her, and each time, she managed to act as if nothing they did fazed her.

She felt in her heart that a lot of the flak she was getting from the girls was because of Supreme and she hated him for that. She hated the very sight of him and hated even more when he spoke to her, for she knew that his very actions could lead to her being punished by the girls who liked him.

Unlike most boys his age, Supreme enjoyed reading and then "dropping knowledge" as he called it about what he read. He could go on for what seemed like days about politics, religion, history, love, life, sports and, just about any other topic anyone would come up with. He was smart, but far from a nerd. Beneath his nice guy persona lived a young man who had little fear and would fight when provoked or threatened.

He had only been in a few fights in his young life, but his victories were so impressive and decisive that everyone knew not to mess with him. His parents raised him not to start fights, but when they were started he had strict instructions to finish them, and finish them he did.

It was rumored that he once got into a fight with one of the local junior college football players who he felt had disrespected one of the elderly ladies in the neighborhood. According to the rumor, it was almost over as fast as it started. One stiff jab, right hook, left hook and a right over the top, and that was all she wrote for his opponent.

Tonya was a loner, so she rarely ever heard any of the rumors about Supreme unless she happened to be sitting close enough to someone who happened to be gossiping about him. Despite her dislike for him, she couldn't help but be intrigued by the things she did hear. When he wasn't looking, she would sneak a peek and occasionally find herself lost in looking at his muscular arms when he wore tank tops.

She had convinced herself that all men were all alike, so she didn't have any time for them or interest in them, until one stormy Friday evening, when Supreme gave her and Raven a ride home from the corner store.

Normally, she would have told him to go to hell but it was raining really badly and Raven was already suffering from a slight summer cold. Immediately upon entering the car, she was on guard for any tricky moves, but Supreme was a perfect gentleman the entire ride.

"So why don't you like me?" he asked suddenly.

"Because you're a boy," she responded with a sharp tone.

"Because I am a boy?" he asked, puzzled at her response.

"Yes, because you're a boy and I know what all boys want."

"And what is that, if I may ask?" asked Supreme, with a curious expression.

"Look, Malik, you're a nice-looking boy, but I really don't have time for boys right now. Plus, my stepfather would kill me if he even knew I was riding in this car with you."

"Yeah, I have heard about that stepfather of yours. He's a piece of work, they say."

Her mind began to wander. Did Supreme know about all the men she had slept with? she wondered. *He has to know*, she thought to herself.

"Stop the car," she demanded.

"What, what did I do?"

"If you think I am going to let you have your way with me, Malik, then you got another thing coming," she furiously stated.

"What in the hell are you talking about, Tonya?"

"I know what you want and I am telling you right now you're not getting it."

"Okay, Tonya. I admit I do like you, but it is not like that. I am not like that."

"Why me? All of the little nappy-headed girls chase behind you like puppies, why not one of them?" she responded with irritation in her voice.

"Because there is something special about you and I want to be a part of it. Not only are you smart, but you are beautiful and so much different than all of the other girls I've met," he continued.

No one had ever told her that she was special, and hearing it coming from Supreme broke her down softly. She did her best not to smile, but inside, her smile was as big and bright as the shine of the sun.

"So what have I ever done to you for you to be so cold toward me?" he asked.

"Because you get me in trouble," she responded, after breaking from her trance. "All of the girls in the school hate me because of you and the more attention you show me, the meaner they are to me. I just want to go to school and..."

"I'm so sorry," he interrupted with a seriously concerned look on his face. "I didn't know," he continued, as he reached for her hand.

After convincing her not to get out of the car, he pulled into an empty parking space along the curb. While Raven sat in his lap, playing with the steering wheel and blowing the horn to her amusement, Supreme and Tonya laughed and talked for what seemed like hours. She hadn't laughed and smiled so hard in all of her life and, for the first time, she realized how much she loved to laugh. Supreme was no comedian, but seeing the enjoyment on her face, he told every joke he could remember. He had never had to work so hard for a girl's attention and time, but, in his heart, he truly felt she was worth it.

# The Sweetest Summer Fall

For the remainder of the summer, Supreme, Tonya and Raven spent every available moment together, but she never let him come by where she lived. He never pressured her on it, almost as if he knew why she never invited him over or allowed him to visit. He never said a word about it and, as the summer days passed, they grew closer and closer. Seeing him was the highlight of her days and slowly, her self-esteem and confidence started to rise from beneath the ashes.

At Supreme's advice, she had learned to stand up to the girls who had been bullying her for years. "People will always pick on you until you stand up for yourself," he told her. And that's exactly what she did.

The next time she saw Angela, without warning, she drew back as far as she could and swung her history book forward, smashing it against the side of her face. The impact of the book knocked her off her feet and against the lockers that lined the hall way. The other girls stood in shock as Tonya drew back to deliver a second blow with her fist. Her knuckles connected to the corner of her eye and the third blow connected with the side of her jaw. Angela's plea for mercy stopped her in mid-swing. Tonya stared down upon her, breathing heavily with her arm cocked back ready to deliver another hard punch to her head.

"If you ever bother me again, the next time I swear, there will be no mercy," she screamed at her before walking away.

The crowd of students that had gathered to watch the fight parted like the Red Sea as Tonya walked up the hallway towards the school exit. She was a nervous wreck, but felt good about what she had done. She had just defeated her arch nemesis that had plagued her for far too long. When she made it to the door and saw her reflection in the glass, a huge smile spread across her face. She was proud of herself for the first time in her life.

Just before she made it to the building that housed the school childcare services, she stopped by the bathroom to compose herself. She was still trembling from the fight and slightly out of breath. She put some water on her face, straightened her clothes in the mirror and headed to her daughter's classroom as if nothing had happened.

Later that day, she told Supreme about what she did and they both laughed as she described the look on Angela's face when she stared down on her after the fight. He was proud of her for standing up for herself and, from his own personal experiences, he knew that no one would be bothering her again at school.

The following week Supreme invited her and Raven to attend church with him and his parents the following Sunday. He explained that after church, most of his family met at his parent's house for Sunday dinner and that he would love for her to join them.

She had never gone to church and the idea of meeting his parents scared her to death. She felt unworthy and inferior and quickly made up an excuse for why she would not be able to join them for church or dinner. *I don't even have anything to wear*, she thought to herself, but by the end of the school week, he was able to convince her to come, despite her reservation.

"Come as you are and it does not matter what you wear," he told her.

Supreme liked Tonya more than she knew and he was excited about her meeting his parents.

The day before she was supposed to attend church with the Robertson's, she waited for her parents to leave before sneaking out of the house herself. With Raven in her arms, she made her way down to the shopping center where all of the clothing stores were located. She walked up and down the sidewalk, looking through the windows at the dresses in the different shops until she spotted one she liked. After making her way inside the store, she pretended to browse around, looking at blouses and dresses in her size.

She was nervous, but as soon as the ladies in the store were distracted by other customers, she took the dress she had been looking at and stuffed it in Raven's baby bag that she had draped over her shoulder. Before anyone could notice, she walked out of the door as fast as her legs could carry her. Her heart was beating fast in her chest, as she hurried up the sidewalk.

"Ma'am, ma'am," she heard a man shouting behind her.

She was too afraid to look back. She could see the shadow of the person pursuing her coming up fast behind her. Before she could make the turn around the corner, she felt a large hand grab her shoulder. *I'm going to jail,* she thought to herself. Her mind began to race as she turned around to face the man who had stopped her. To her surprise, he had a puzzled look on his face.

"I think this belongs to you," he said, as he held out one of Raven's shoes.

In her haste, she didn't even notice that one of Raven's shoes had fallen off outside of the store.

"You sure can walk fast. I almost had to run to catch you," he continued.

"I'm so sorry, Sir, I didn't realize it was me you were calling out to," she responded with a sigh of relief.

After thanking the man, she made her way to the bus stop and back home where she laid the dress out on the bed to admire it. She sat Raven down on the bed and quickly undressed so she could try it on. She stared at herself in the mirror in amazement at how pretty the dress looked on her. Her smile was a big as the sun as she twirled around like a ballerina in front of the mirror. Raven watched on in excitement at the bright yellow dress twirling around in the air.

Tonya woke up early Sunday morning to find the house was empty, as she had hoped. She was extremely nervous about going to church and meeting Supreme's parents and, for a quick second, she thought about backing out. She pushed the thought out of her mind, as she knew how disappointed he would be.

Her low self-esteem made it easy for her fears and self-doubt to get the best of her, which, in turn, made her feel inferior. In her mind, she felt that she was not good enough for Supreme and his family.

*What am I doing*, she wondered, as she paced about the house. *I don't know anything about church or having dinner with people like that. I can't go through with this.*

She sat beside the bed with her head in her hands. She sat there for nearly an hour, going back forth in her head about what she should do before she finally made up her mind to go.

Supreme had been nothing but nice to her and she felt she at least owed him the decency of showing up as she had promised. It was nearly 9:00 AM when she finished getting dressed. She dressed Raven and they made their way to the bus stop she had told him to pick her up at. When she reached the bus stop, he was already there waiting, with a huge smile on his face. When he saw them coming, he quickly jumped out of the car and made his way around to the passenger side and opened the door for them like the gentlemen he was.

"You both look so pretty today," he said, as they got into the car.

Once he was sure they were securely inside, he rushed back around to the driver's side and they headed off to church.

By the time they arrived at the church, the parking lot was full and cars were lined up and down the road leading up to it. He found the closest parking space he could and pulled in. Tonya's was extremely nervous and her palms were sweating as she extended her hand to him so that he could assist her getting out of the car.

As they got closer to the church, she noticed a woman standing at entrance watching them as they approached. She knew immediately from the way the woman was looking at them that she had to be his mother. The woman wore an expensive-looking white dress with intricate crystals and small flowers across the bust that connected in the back. She was the same complexion as Supreme and shared his big, bright smile.

"Mom, I would like for you to meet my girlfriend, Tonya," he said when they were within speaking distance. "Tonya, this is my mother, Mrs. Sarah Robertson."

"Oooh, it's so good to finally meet you," she said to Tonya, as she leaned forward embracing her with a warm, Southern hug. "I've heard so much about you. How are you? And who is the pretty, little, young lady you have with you?

"It's a pleasure to meet you, Mrs. Robertson Tonya responded, with nervousness in her voice. "This is my daughter, Raven".

"Raven, now isn't that a pretty name, fitting for a pretty, little girl," Mrs. Robertson said.

Supreme stood back with a huge smile on his face as his mother took Raven into her arms, grabbed Tonya by the hand and led them into the church. Tonya was amazed by the beauty of the church and the elegant hand carved oak benches that filled the room. Everyone inside was dressed in their best clothes and there were fresh flowers all throughout the church.

Just inside the church entrance, they were met by a man who looked like the older version of Supreme. He looked to be in his early 40's, but he was obviously in good shape, just as his son was. After a brief introduction, he led them to the front of the church, where they took a seat on the front row near the piano. Mrs. Robertson sat next to her husband with Raven in her lap and she motioned for Tonya to sit right next to her and Supreme sat on the other side.

The church procession started with a call to worship and then, a prayer. Sensing Tonya was unfamiliar with the program, Mrs. Robertson took special care to make sure she felt comfortable by talking her through everything. Early into the procession, Raven fell asleep in Mrs. Robertson's arms. Midway through the service, the choir, led by a heavyset, young man began to sing.

"This song is called 'God Is'," Mrs. Robertson whispered to Tonya.

As the words of the classic gospel tune floated through the church, Tonya felt a slight chill move through her body. She looked around to see if there was a window open, but all of the windows were closed. The sound of the man's voice almost brought her to tears. She gritted her teeth together tightly to keep from crying. Seeing her becoming emotional, Mrs. Robertson reached over and placed her hand on top of hers and gently patted it while whispering, "It's going to be alright."

After the choir finished, a man wearing a black, tailored suit stepped up to the podium. He began to speak to the churchgoers in a calm voice as he scanned over the pages of the book that was in front of him. The more he spoke, the louder his voice became and the louder his voice rose, the more excited with joy he became.

The people in attendance would shout aloud "Amen" and "Preach" when he said something they agreed with. After about 20 minutes of speaking from the book, his voice could be heard in every corner of the church. Sweat beads began to pour from his head as he shouted the words of his sermon to the congregation.

"Can I get an amen from somebody?" he shouted to the audience and nearly the entire church answered simultaneously.

By the time the Preacher's reached the end of his sermon, the flood of tears that had been forming in Tonya's eyes could no longer be held back. She had so many emotions built up inside of her and the words of the Preacher and the sound of the choir touched home. She didn't make a sound as the tears rolled down her cheeks one by one onto her dress. Mr. Robertson took a handkerchief from his pocket and handed it to her as Supreme moved closer to her and wrapped his arms around her shoulder to comfort her. He held her this way until the service was over.

After meeting and greeting several members of the church, they all made their way to their cars. Tonya barely spoke as Supreme followed his parents' car back to the house. Before going inside, he asked her if she was okay.

"I'm fine," she said, with a smile.

They both got out of the car and joined his parents, who were waiting for them inside.

When they entered the house, they found Mr. Robertson setting the table and Mrs. Robertson bringing out the dishes of food she had cooking while they were in church. Tonya had never seen so much food all laid out at one time. On the table, there was deep fried chicken, golden buttermilk biscuits, baked macaroni and cheese, fried okra, greens, candied yams, corn bread, and sun-baked Southern lemon sweet tea.

There was a small dessert table along the wall, upon which were two cakes and a fresh baked sweet potato pie. She had not eaten anything for breakfast and her stomach growled at the sight of the food. Raven had been asleep since church, but the smell of the food had her fully awake.

She had become accustomed to school lunch being her best meal of the day, but now, before her, was a feast of food, food that she had only seen pictures of, but never had a chance to try. When the food was on the table, they all circled the table holding hands, as Mr. Robinson led them in saying grace.

"Dear God, we gather here today, as a family, to give thanks for the food and blessings you have bestowed upon us.

Please let this food be nourishing to our mind, body and soul. We ask oh merciful Father that you continue to bless us and keep us strong as a family. In your name, we pray. Amen."

After blessing the food, Supreme pulled up a chair between where he and Tonya were sitting and they all took their seats. As they filled their bellies with food, Mr. Robertson took the opportunity to tell Tonya every war story he could remember. Tonya was captivated by his words and tales of heroic action. She listened intensely as he told her about the time he was shot as they tried to take a position on a hillside during Vietnam the war. The more stories he told, the more animated he grew.

"Honey," Mrs. Robertson interrupted. "I think she has heard enough of your war stories. Give the child a break." Everyone at the table laughed, though Mr. Robertson looked a little embarrassed.

After dinner, Tonya helped Mrs. Robertson clear the table to make room for dessert. The food was delicious, but she had been looking forward to getting a slice of the chocolate cake. Supreme cut her a huge slice and then, he cut a smaller slice for Raven, who too was eager to get a taste of the cake. While everyone used their forks to eat the cake, she used her hands. They all looked at her in amusement as she got cake all over her face and in her hair. The Robertson's hadn't had a baby in the house since Supreme was a baby himself and it was obvious that they were enjoying every minute of having Raven around.

Shortly after finishing dessert, Tonya knew it was time for her to get home. She had the time of her life spending the day with the Robertson's, but the entire time, in the back of her mind, she knew that she would have to go back to her reality at the end of the day. She said her goodbyes and hugged Mr. and Mrs. Robertson before walking out of the door and to the car. Supreme's parents stood in the doorway of their home, embracing each other while waving as Supreme backed the car out of the driveway and headed up the street.

For the short period of time, Tonya was in heaven. Everything was starting to look up for her. Her social life was now in repair and, by summer's end, she was head over heels in love with Supreme and vice versa. Even Raven had grown attached to him. But the fairy tale was disrupted when he broke the bad news to both of them.

He had enlisted in the US Army and would be shipping off to basic training in October. The thought of him leaving hit her like a brick to the chest. Her world stood still as he attempted to explain his decision to join the service. She prayed that this was just another one of his jokes, but the punch line never came. She wanted to cry, but she held her tears and smiled as if she was happy for him.

"Congrats on your decision to join the Army," she managed to say while trying to keep the tears from flooding her eyes.

He swore on his honor as a man that he would return for her and Raven once he got settled, but she knew that once he left, he would forget all about her and be gone forever.

"I promise I am going to write you every week," he explained, as the large teardrops began to run down her face.

She had held them back as long as she could, but her emotions were now getting the best of her. He instinctively moved in to comfort her by placing his arm around her shoulder. He held her and Raven tight for a few minutes.

"I am doing this for us," he said, after a few moments of silence.

Tonya was having a hard time understanding how leaving her was in her best interest.

"I know you are," she responded, with a twinge of disbelief in her tone.

For the next few months, she religiously received letters from Supreme once a week, just as he promised, but all of a sudden, the letters stopped coming.

She wrote him six more letters without a single response. Her heart ached with disappointment, but she blamed herself for being stupid enough to buy into the dreams of the two of them living happily ever after. Days turned to weeks and weeks to months and not a single letter arrived from Supreme. She once stood by the mailbox awaiting the postman, but now she hated to see him coming. The mere sight of the postman reminded her of him. She missed him dearly and she felt as if she physically ached from the loneliness. He was her first and only love and she was having a hard time getting him out of her system.

It had been eight months since he left for the Army and five months had passed since she received his last letter. He told her that his basic training would only be two months and then, he had to go to school to learn the job he would be doing in the Army. That should have lasted only four months, but there was still no sign from Supreme.

It was the summer of 1989 and she was soon to turn 18. Raven was now three-years-old and full of life. She reflected back over her life and grew sad at the thought of how tragic it had been thus far.

The only highlight she could think of was Raven and Supreme coming into her life. She had been beaten and caged like an animal. She had been used and traded for drugs and money by her own parents most of her life. She had endured being bullied and spat on by her fellow students at school. Now, more than ever, even more than when her stepfather was raping her and pimping her out to support their drug habit, she thought of running away again, but she simply didn't have anywhere to go.

*If only Supreme would have stayed true to his word, I wouldn't have to worry about this*, she thought to herself.

She had stopped worrying about what was happening to her and had come to accept the misfortunes of her life, but she was now worried about Raven. Several of the johns had started asking about Raven, but her stepfather would always say that she was too young, but check back in a couple of years.

"She is going to be a whore just like her momma," he would say, with that sick grin plastered on his face.

The thought of harm coming to Raven pushed Tonya to move her plans for escape up sooner than originally planned.

# This I Will Defend

It was the morning of her birthday when she awakened to find Raven missing from her side. She sprang from the bed in panic and began searching the room and then, the rest of the house.

When she reached her mother's room, she found her stepfather lying in the bed next to Raven. Tonya rushed over to her as fast as she could and immediately began inspecting her for signs of harm.

"What did you do to her, you sick bastard?" she screamed at her stepfather. "If you hurt her, I swear I'm going to kill you."

"I didn't do anything to the little crying bitch, yet, but she is going to have to start kicking in around here. A pretty little girl like that can bring in a pretty penny, if you know what I mean," he said, with a smile on his face. "Sooner or later, I am going to have to sample the goods before I sell it."

Before he could say another word, Tonya ran out of the room with Raven in her arms. She had to get out of that house and think for a minute. Just as she walked towards the door to leave, there was a knock. She opened the door and was shocked to find Supreme standing there on her doorstep with a handful of flowers and a huge smile on his face.

She wanted to be angry, but she was so happy to see him that a smile broke through the frown on her face to greet him.

"Who the fuck is that at my door?" her stepfather yelled from the bedroom.

Before she could respond, he was standing behind her at the door in an instant.

"Nigga, what the fuck do you want?" he yelled, staring directly at Supreme.

The smile on Supreme's face was immediately replaced by a serious and stern look.

"I am here to see Tonya," he responded in a low, even voice.

"To see Tonya?" Well I hope you got some money or some dope because Tonya ain't fucking for free," he barked.

Seeing the confused look on Supreme face, Tonya tried to guide him away from the house, but her stepfather grabbed her by the arm.

"Where the fuck do you think you're going, Miss Hot-in-the-Ass?"

In an instant, Supreme pushed through the door and grabbed him by the throat.

"Don't you ever fucking touch her again," he whispered in his ear. "I have heard about you and if you so much as look at her the wrong way, I will cut your fucking eyes out."

Slick trembled in fright as Supreme squeezed his hands tighter around his neck to make his point. Tonya stood in shock and amazement at how swift Supreme moved in to protect her.

Then, as if the incident had never happened, Supreme turned towards Tonya and asked in a calm voice, "Where would my ladies like to go for breakfast?"

A huge smile spread across Tonya's face, as she scooped Raven up into her arms and followed him out of the door. She paused for a moment when she spotted his brand new, all-back Ford Expedition. Like the true gentlemen she remembered, Supreme opened the door for her and held it until his ladies were sitting secure in their seats.

Over breakfast, Supreme explained to her why he wasn't able to write. He was part of a Special Forces Counter Insurgent team that deployed to Iraq for a 12-month tour. He went on to explain that shortly after he completed his Advanced Individual Training at Fort Benning, Georgia, he attended a Special Forces recruiting session and decided to give it a try. Before he attended the Special Forces course, he had to complete the airborne school, air assault school, ranger school and several other military schools, which he did always at the top of his class. He had left home as a boy and star athlete and returned a man and a warrior.

She was relieved to know that he had not met up with another woman and forgotten about her, but she wasn't getting her hopes up this time.

"So, how long are you in town?" she asked.

"I am on leave for about 3 weeks, but I don't plan on being here that long. I just came to see my family and to get you and Raven," he said.

A nervous feeling overcame her.

"Say what? Are you serious?" she asked with wide eyes.

"You still love me, don't you?"

"Yes, I still love you. You're the only man I have ever loved, but I think there are some things you need to know about me."

You mean that back at the house?"

"Yes, and –"

"Say no more," he said, placing his hand on hers. I have always known about that and I don't care about your past. You're my woman now and no one will ever harm you again. I have been waiting an entire year to tell you how much I love you."

He paused for a second, as if he was trying to collect himself. Then, he leaned back, reached into his pocket and pulled out a large diamond ring.

"So, will you do me the honor and be my forever and last breath."

Raven looked on in confusion, as tears started to roll down her mother's face.

"YES!" she yelled. "YES! I will!"

"Well, give me a kiss, woman," he said, with a smile.

The two kissed for what felt like hours.

"Now, that we have gotten that out of the way, I don't want you to stay at your family's house tonight. I don't want to have to kill that man."

"Okay, I just need to go back and pack our things."

"Alright, well, you can drop me off at my mother's house and take my car."

After dropping Supreme off, she had a bright smile on her face as she and her daughter headed back to the house that she hated so much. When she reached the house, there were two cars parked in front of the house. As she walked in, she could hear two men arguing and one of the voices sounded like that of her stepfather. She walked in the room to find two men standing over her stepfather, who was sitting in a chair, looking terrified. Her mother emerged from out of nowhere and pushed her into the room in sight of the two men.

"There she is," her stepfather said, pointing in her direction.

The two men turned around and that was when she realized that the two men were the Thompson brothers.

Out of all the johns that came to the house for her, she hated them the most. Most johns came and handled their business and left, but not these two.

They enjoyed watching each other beat and choke a woman while having their way with them. Her stepfather walked over to her with an angry look on his face and backhanded her to the floor.

"Where the hell have you been, bitch?" he shouted.

She jumped from the floor and grabbed Raven before attempting to back out of the room. Her mother blocked the doorway and prevented their escape.

"You need to get your ass in there and take care of business," her mother screamed.

Before she could respond, one of the men hit her from the blind side with a right cross. She was dazed and could barely make out the words coming from her mother and the two men. From what she could understand, her stepfather had received some drugs from the men as pre-payment for sexual favors with her and Raven.

The sound of Raven's name gave her strength to get up, but she was quickly knocked back down to the floor by a hard blow to the head. After a few more words with her mother, the men dragged her into the bedroom, along with Raven, who was now crying.

She had barely regained consciousness to see one of the men undressing Raven. She struggled to get up from the bed, but fell to the floor. As she made her second attempt to get up, she saw the bedroom door open slowly. Like a ghost, Supreme slid in the room, unnoticed by the men until he was right up on them.

He wheeled a blade like an artist with a paint brush. With one quick, lunging move, he imbedded the knife into one of the men's chest. The other man reached for his gun, but he was to slow.

Supreme sprung from the bed in a driving motion with his arm extended, knife in hand. The first slash went across the man's stomach, which caused him to collapse to the floor. Without mercy, Supreme brought the next one across his throat.

Supreme finished his motion in a martial arts stance, as if he expected more men to come running towards him. Without even so much as a glimpse in Tonya's direction, he moved back through the door from which he came. Tonya grabbed Raven and followed.

They stopped when they heard noises coming from the living room closet. Supreme pulled a large pistol from the small of his back and took aim. The door flung open, exposing Tonya's mother and stepfather hiding in the closet.

Supreme handed the gun over to Tonya and walked out of the room with Raven. When he returned with a large can of gasoline, Tonya was taking aim. She squeezed the trigger and two loud explosions lit the room in a bright flash of light.

The two slugs jolted her stepfather against the closet wall. Before her mother could scream, another bullet pierced her skull. Tonya dropped the gun and stood in shock at what she had done.

Supreme moved in and directed her to take Raven outside and wait for him.

"When you see the flames, run to a neighbor's house and call the police. Tell them you don't know what happened. You just woke up and the house was on fire and you escaped as fast as you could," he said, firmly.

At the command of her fiancé's voice, Tonya moved, without hesitation, out of the front door and across the street.

Moments later, she saw Supreme running from the back of the house as flames started to spread over the house.

She had always wanted to kill her parents, but never imagined Supreme would be a part of it. It was 11 in the morning, as Tonya and Raven stood in silence, watching the flames stretch into the early morning sky. As she stood in the street, she thought about all the pain and suffering she had endured while living there. All of the beatings, sex abuse and torture were now up in flames. The people responsible for so much of her pain were now dead and she smiled at the thought of starting a new beginning with her hero and warrior.

The sound of the sirens in the distance snapped her out of the daze and she began thinking about what she would say. Supreme had left the scene and she would rather die than betray him.

The fire engine turned the corner in blazing speed and came to a quick stop. The fire fighters jumped from the truck and into action like a well-rehearsed team. One tall, older man stood in front of the burning house and shouted instructions to the others.

"Get the hose hooked up!"
"Timmy, get one of your guys around to the back of the house and see if anyone is inside!"

"Jeff, get your team ready to breach the front door on my command."

With a simple nod of acknowledgment, the men moved without hesitation.

The guy who seemed to be in charged noticed Tonya and Raven standing across the street and walked over in their direction.

"Ma'am, is this your house?" he asked.

"Yes, sir," she answered.

"Do you know if anyone is in the house?"

"I'm not sure. I woke up and the house was on fire. I grabbed my daughter and ran out as fast as I could."

"Okay, just wait right here until the police arrives," he said, as he turned his attention back to his men, who were now spraying water on the house.

On his command, they kicked the front door in and, in a single file line, entered the burning house. Suddenly, the men rushed back out of the house. The house was now fully engulfed in flames.

"Chief, if there is someone in the house, they're definitely not alive now," one of the fire fighters yelled.

# Newly Born

The following day, Detective Franklin was assigned as the lead homicide investigator on the case. He was infamously known to be a crooked cop in the streets, but throughout the department, he was known to be one of the best homicide detectives in the police department. From the moment he read over the case file, he knew that there was more to the story than what had been told to the on-scene investigator.

Later that day, he found Tonya, who was now staying with the Robertson's. She was sitting on the porch when he arrived at the house. Before he could get out of the car, she started to make her way down the walkway, meeting him halfway. She stood stone-faced as he began to question her.

"So, tell me what happened at the house"
"I've already given my statement to the other cop," she responded with a sharp tone.
"Yes, you did, but now I want you to tell me what happened with a little less attitude," he replied, now obviously agitated by her snapping demeanor.

"Okay, I'll tell you again. When I was just a child, a dirty pedophile cop came by my house on several occasions and had sex with me. I finally ended up using his gun to try and kill myself after he had finished with me. I'm sure the hospital still has the police-issued bullet that was pulled from my chest. For all I know, that crooked cop killed my parents and set the house on fire to cover up his tracks. Now, is there anything else you would like to know, Detective Franklin?" she asked, her face blank and emotionless.

Franklin, with a stunned look on his face, stood frozen in place, his eyes wide and mouth slightly open. In that instant, he realized who the young lady was that stood before him.

His mind quickly shifted back to the night that he tried so hard to distance himself from. He saw his entire life crashing and burning right before his very eyes.

*If anyone finds out that my gun was used by that little girl, my life is over. I could be linked to these murders and do some serious jail time,* he thought.

The thought of going to jail terrified him and he began backing away from her. She kept her unblinking eyes locked on him the entire way.

"That'll be all, Miss," he mumbled.

He jumped back in his car as fast as he could and sped away. That was the last Tonya ever heard from Detective Franklin. Two weeks later, the fire and police department investigators concluded that the murders and fire was a result of a drug deal gone wrong. Tonya was subsequently cleared of any implications and shortly after, they loaded all of their worldly belongings into Supreme's Ford Expedition and never looked back again.

But, before they hit the road, she stopped where the house once stood and left a dozen, dead roses to symbolize the end of a love that never was.

# About the Author

I would like to sincerely thank and acknowledge a lot of great people who helped or inspired me to write this book but before I thank them please allow me to give honor and praise to the most-high God Almighty for blessing me with an unconquerable soul, a good heart, strong mind, powerful spirit and life.

My Grandmothers, Ida Lee Windham and Sarah Catherine Wright, thanks for loving me and raising me as your own. You didn't have to but you did and I'm forever grateful.

My three children, you are my inspiration and the best thing about me. I love each of you more than I love life itself! D-Roc, you have an incredible spirit that inspires me and I love you just as I love my very own.

To avoid missing and offending anyone I would like to give a special thanks to all of my family, friends and everyone else who took the time to give me an encouraging word of support! Bob Rousseau thanks so much for your subject matter expertise in writing this book.

To my beloved fraternity, Omega Psi Phi and all Greek Letter Orgs you inspire me to want to be great through your continued efforts of service to others.

Thanks in advance to everyone who supported me by purchasing this book.